MIGO & ALI

- A-Z of ISLAM -

Zanib Mian

Illustrated by

Basma Hossam

Contents

Introduction

This book has been lovingly written, to offer simple explanations of Islamic words and topics to young children. It has taken over a year to research. The content of each topic has been carefully considered, to convey material to a young reader, at a level that they will grasp and retain.

There are no depictions of any of the prophets or sahaba (peace and blessings be upon them) in this book. The content was written with reference to many sources; only material that can be backed by sahih hadith or the Qur'an has been included.

May Allah reward Ustadh Yusuf Chaudhary for checking the content of this book for accuracy. We ask for great reward also, for each of the other scholars who were directly or indirectly consulted for research purposes. Ameen.

Abbreviations and their meanings:

saw - stands for Sal Allahu Alayhi Wasalam/ May Allah's peace and blessings be upon him.
as - Stands for alayhi salaam, or alaihim salaam/ Upon him (or them) be peace.

ra - stands for Radi Allah An / May Allah be pleased with him or her.

MIGO & ALI

- A-Z of ISLAM -

Adhaan

The adhaan is what Muslims say out loud to call everyone to pray. You've heard it lots of times before, at the mosque, on the television, or at home.

It is said in a beautiful voice, by the mu'adhin (see Mu'adhin). It let's everyone know that it's time to pray and that they should all come to do their salah together.

Allahu akbar, Allahu akbar, Allahu akbar;

an laa ilaaha ill-Allah,

an laa ilaaha ill-Allah,

hadu anna Muhammadan rasool-Allah,

hadu anna Muhammadan rasool-Allah,

hayya 'ala al-salaah, hayya 'ala al-salaah;

hayya 'ala'l-falaah, hayya 'ala'l-falaah;

Allahu akbar, Allahu akbar;

Laa ilaaha ill-Allah.

The first adhaan ever, was given by **Bilal (ra)**, who was a companion of the Prophet (saw). That was in *Madinah* and Bilal's (ra) words were heard all through the city.

Everyone came quickly and happily to pray together.

Migo: Do you know when you first heard the adhaan, Ali?

Ali: When?

Migo: When you were born!

Ali: No way!? Was I born in a masjid?

Migo: Hahaha. No, my silly berry nut juice, you were born in a hospital, but when a little Muslim baby is born, no matter where they are born, someone gives the adhaan in his or her tiny little ear. It's the first thing the baby hears.

Ali: Wow, Migo! Maybe that's why I love the adhaan!

Migo: It sure could be!

When you hear the adhaan, the best thing that you could do is to listen very quietly to it, and say the words of the adhaan gently, in a whisper, just like the mu'adhin is saying them. But when he says,

"Hayya 'ala al-salaah (come to prayer)"
and
"hayya 'ala'l-falaah (come to success)."

you should say:

La hawla wa la quwwata illa billah (There is no might or power except Allah's).

When the adhaan has finished, you should make this dua, because if you do, the Prophet (saw) is going to ask Allah to give you Jannah!

Allahumma hadhihi al-da'wat al-taammah wa al-salaat al-qaa'imah ati Muhammadan al-waseelata wa al-fadee-lata waba'th hu maqaaman mahmudan alladhee wa'adta.

Alhamdulillah

Alhamdulillah are words in Arabic that we say to thank Allah for His blessings. It means that all thanks and praise is for Allah.

Allah loves people who thank Him, and He gives them more and more!

When we say Alhamdulillah, we say it because we know that **all good things come from Allah**, and He is the one we should be thanking. We say it because we admire Allah, and we love Him. We say Alhamdulillah from the bottom of our hearts to show that we are very happy that He's with us and giving us all these blessings.

We should say Alhamdulillah all the time, because it brings us lots of reward and blessing from Allah.

Ali: Does that mean I don't have to say thank you next time you bring me cake? I only have to say thank you to Allah?

Migo: No, cheeky button! Islam teaches us good manners and to be thankful to others. So you would still thank me, because I did something nice for you, but you can also say Alhamdulillah for the cake, because if Allah hadn't made me, or made it possible for me to bring you the cake, you wouldn't have it.

Ali: OK Migo. Thank you for telling me that. Alhamdulillah you told me that.

Migo: Haha. Good boy.

Ali: We say Alhamdulillah when we burp and sneeze too!

Migo: Yes. Guess what? Allah likes sneezes and sneezing is good for us! So when we sneeze, we thank Allah by saying Alhamdulillah. And if you hear a person sneeze and then say 'Alhamdulillah', you should say 'Yarhamuk Allah (may Allah have mercy on you).'

Ali: And I guess Shaytan doesn't like sneezes!

Migo: No, but he likes yawns!

Ali: Haha, because yawns are lazy! But why did you

say Alhamdulillah when you had a headache the other day, Migo?"

Migo: Ah! Because, even a headache is a blessing from Allah. Everything that happens to us, is. I don't know why having a headache that day was a blessing for me, but I know that Allah knows, and I

trust Him. For example, it could be that if I didn't have a headache, I might have chosen to go out and I might have slipped on a banana skin when I went out.

Ali: Wow. I am going to say Alhamdulillah all the time now and for everything!

Migo: Me too!

Allah

Allah is the Arabic word for God. There is only one Allah. There are no other gods. He doesn't have a mother or a father, or any sons or daughters. That's because He is not like us, or any of His creation. We should only worship Allah and nothing else.

Allah made everything - the mountains, trees, birds, the plants, us, and everything else. He can do anything! He is the most powerful. Nothing can happen without Him. He was always there. He sees everything and He knows everything.

Allah has *99 names*, but the names He most wants us to know him by are **AR-RAHMAN** and **AR-RAHEEM**, the **MOST COMPASSIONATE**, the **MOST MERCIFUL**. That means He cares a lot about how we feel and understands us very well. He also forgives us and doesn't want us to go through anything bad.

That's because Allah loves us seventy times more than our own mothers.

In Islam, we talk directly to Allah, we don't have to talk to Him through anyone else. *Anyone can talk to Allah, and He always listens and watches.*

ALi: OK, wait Migo! I'm just going to go and tell Allah something.

Migo: You can tell Him here! If it's a big secret, you can speak to Him in your heart, He can still hear you, you know.

Ali: Oh! I thought I had to go and sit on my prayer mat.

Migo: No, my moon dust, anyone can talk to Allah and they can do it wherever they are or whatever they are doing.

Ali: And in what language?

Migo: In any language! Allah understands all the languages in the universe.

Ali: And does Allah have powers?

Migo: Yes, of course He does. He has all the powers! He sees and knows everything that's happening everywhere and He has the power to control all things, big and small.

Ali: Even big like you, Migo?

Migo: Haha, even big like me. Even big like aeroplanes, or hurricanes, or planets and stars!

Ali: Wow, wow, wow, I want to know more about Allah. What does He look like?

Migo: Like nothing in the world you've ever seen before!

Ali: Does He ever get bored?

Migo: Never ever, my treacle tart. Humans get bored, but Allah isn't like a human. So He doesn't need to eat or sleep or get bored or any other stuff that humans do. He is simply amazing. He provides for us, watches over us, protects us, and loves us.

Ali: Alhamdulillah!
I love Allah!

Migo: Me too!

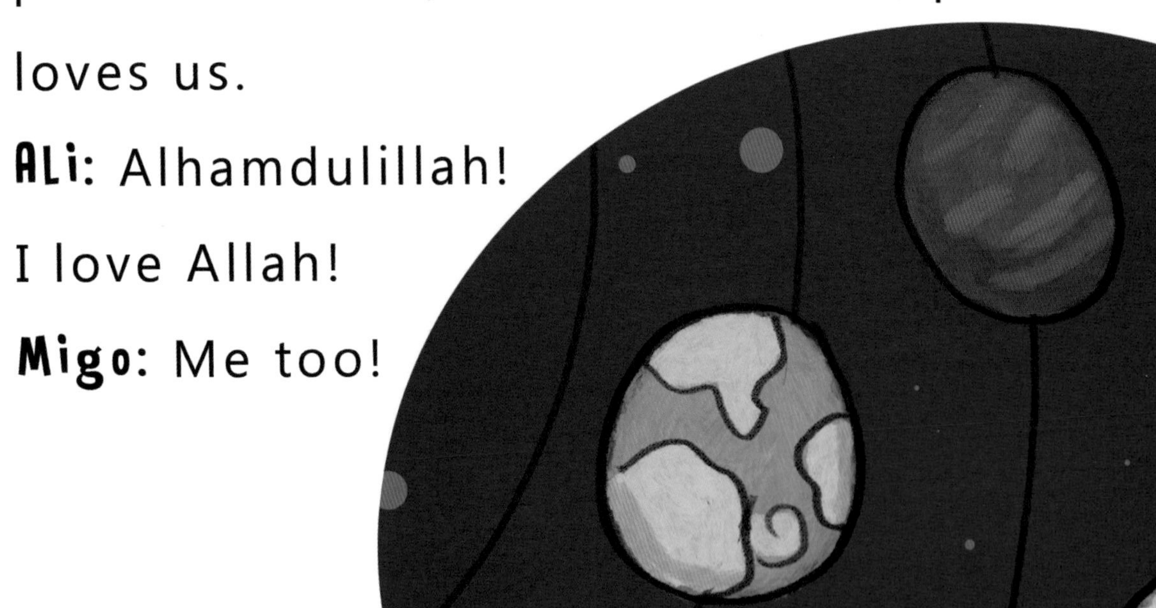

Angels

Angels are wonderful creatures, *made by Allah*. They are amazing! Allah made us from **clay**, but He made angels from **light**. Angels are very different to us. **They can only do good things, no bad things at all. They do exactly what Allah tells them to.**

There are so many angels in outer space that there's not one bit of it where there isn't an angel. And because all of them are saying things to praise Allah, the whole of space sounds like it's shaking.

Ali: Like when we go to the masjid on Eid, and there's nowhere to step, because each space has a person in it?

Migo: Haha, yes exactly like that! Except maybe the angels didn't have to take their shoes off in a big sea of shoes at the door.

Ali: That's because angels don't wear shoes, right Migo?

Migo: Right, my pumpkin butter.

Ali: Are the angels boring, and all exactly the same?

Migo: Is it boring to have 600 wings?

Ali: Wow! Is that true? They have 600 wings?

Migo: When the Prophet (saw) saw Jibreel (as), he said that he was so big that he was filling up the space all the way from the ground to the sky and that he has six hundred wings. But angels come in different sizes. Some have two wings, and some have more, but they all have wings. They are beautiful and strong.

Ali: How strong? Is it like when Superman lifts planes and things? Can angels do that?

Migo: Hahaha. A plane is nothing, my toffee apple! Lifting a plane for some angels, is like lifting an ant for me. Angel Jibreel (as) can knock over a whole city with the tip of one of his wings. Angels can crush mountains. Anyway, angels are real and Superman is made up.

ALi: Angel Jibreel is amazing!

Migo: Yes, Jibreel (as) is the most important angel. He was the first living, breathing creature of Allah and Adam (as) was the first man. Allah speaks to the four most special angels Himself. Sometimes He might speak to angels Mikail or Israfil through Jibreel, but He always speaks to Jibreel (as) Himself.

Jibreel (as) is the angel that came down to speak to all the prophets, passing on messages from Allah. He is the one that came to Ibrahim (as) when the people were about to throw him in the fire. He was the one that came to Hajar (as) when she was searching for water.

ALi: I wish I could see him!

Migo: Well humans can't see angels, my cherry cupcake. Only when they come in human shape, like when Jibreel (as) came to the prophets.

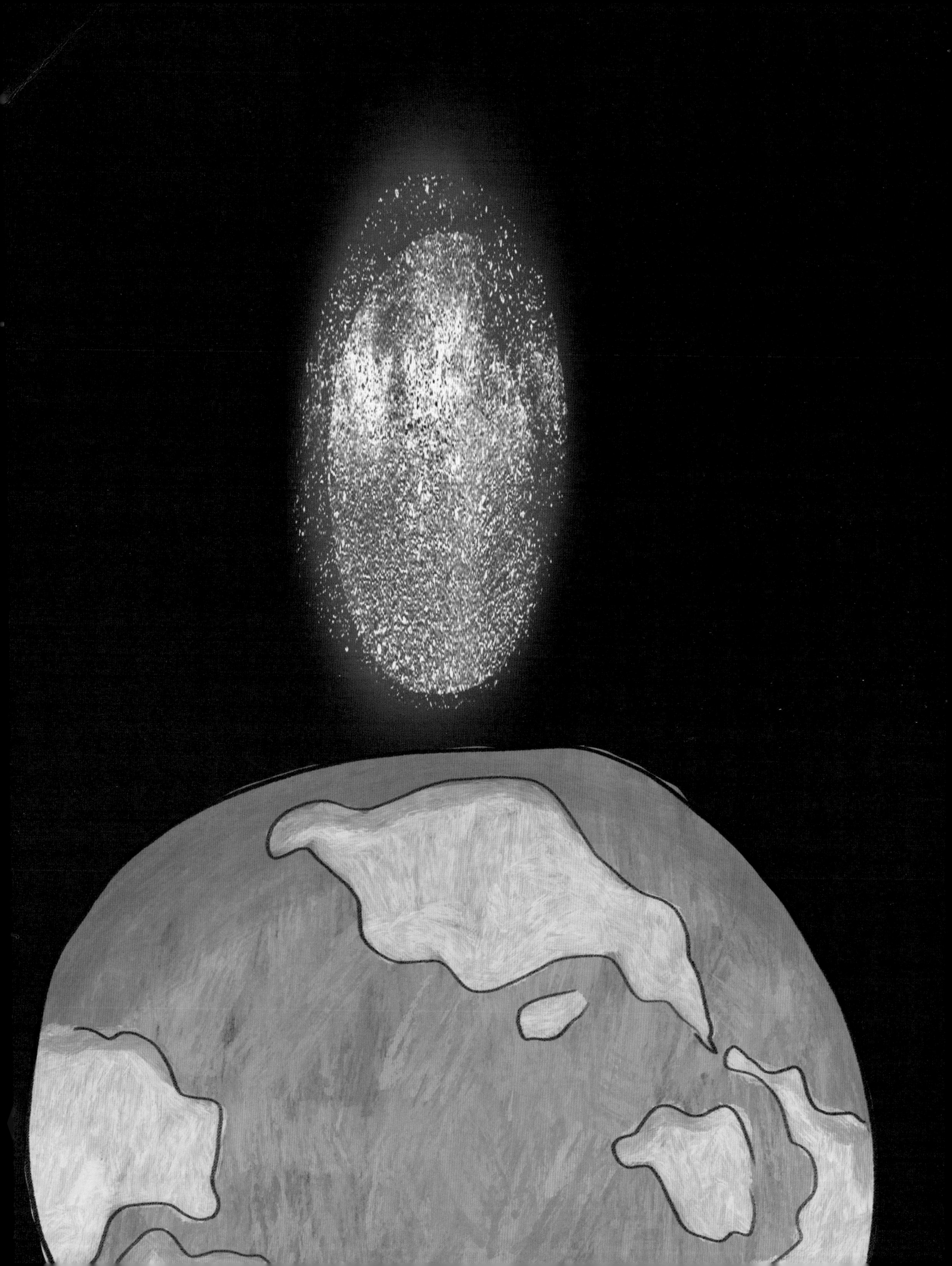

Migo: But you can smell nice for the angels, by always doing good things, because when someone starts thinking about doing a good deed, a beautiful scent starts coming from them, which angels love, and come near to!

Ali: I will! I want them near me!

Migo: Good little rainbow! Did you know that angels are not male or female (girls or boys), they don't eat or sleep and they don't even get tired. And they never get bored! They all have different jobs to do and they love doing them. Look at the rain. Do you know who Allah chose to do that?

Ali: Who?!

Migo: An angel called Mikail (as). He moves the winds and rains and lots more, when Allah tells him to.

Ali: This is totally brilliant, Migo! I'm going to pray now so that angels come near me!

Migo: Haha, OK, my sunshine.

Aqeedah

There are six parts to faith, or imaan, in Islam. That means, if you are a Muslim, you have to believe in all of them and know for sure that they are all true. That is aqeedah.

Those things are:

Belief in Allah – believing that Allah is the one and only God (See Allah).

Belief in Allah's Angels – Angels are magnificent and they're very powerful. We believe in them and we believe that they can only do what Allah has asked them to (see Angels).

Belief in Allah's Books – The Quran is a holy book, which was sent down to the *Prophet Muhammad* (saw). There are other holy books too, the Bible, Torah and Psalms, which were sent to other prophets and messengers. **We believe in all of them.**

Ali: Wait, wait, wait, Migo. If I believe in the Bible, doesn't that make me a Christian and not a Muslim?

Migo: Oh no, my sunshine on a rainy day, Muslims only have to believe that Allah sent books to other prophets and messengers. Those books have been changed by people over the long years, so we don't know which bits of them are from Allah and which bits are made up. The Quran has not changed at all, since it was given to the Prophet Muhammad (saw) so that is the book that we have to use now. If anyone was to say that Allah didn't send a book to the other prophets, that is wrong. But it doesn't mean you are a Christian if you believe that Allah did send Jesus (as) a book.

ALi: Got it!

Belief in Allah's Messengers – In our other book, we learnt all about all the prophets. There was Ibrahim, Musa, Esa (as), and many others. Muslims believe in ALL of Allah's prophets and messengers (see prophets).

Belief in the Last Day – This world isn't forever. As Muslims we believe that. Just like Allah created this world, one day He will make it all end, and we will all go back to Him. Then He will have a look at what we've all been up to in our lives. Whether it was good stuff or bad stuff.

Ali: What about people who have died before the end, Migo? Like my mum's grandma? And my great grandfather? And my great, great grandfather, and my...

Migo: OK, haha, I get it. Stop, stop! Well, those people will come back to life too, to meet Allah.

Ali: Woah! Can Allah do that?

Migo: Of course He can. Allah can do anything you can imagine, and more.

Belief in Divine Destiny- This is believing that Allah knows everything, has power over everything and controls everything. He decides what happens to you, where you will be going, how much money you will have and so on.

Ali: So does that mean that I can't choose to do things myself?

Migo: Yes, you can. Being a human means that we can make choices. But it is up to Allah to allow that choice to happen or not. For example, you might choose to go swimming after lunch. Allah knows that you would have chosen to do that. He might allow you, or might not. If He decides not to allow you then something will happen to stop you from going.

Ali: Then I might feel sad about that, Migo.

Migo: You can, my maple syrup cherry, because you're human. But then you can accept it and get on with other things, because you believe that Allah *chose* for that to happen to you.

Ali: OK, Migo!

Ashura

Ashura is a special day, in a special month called Muharram. Muharram is one of the four holy months and Ashura is on the 10th day (see Islamic months).

On this day, many, many years ago, Allah **SAVED MUSA (AS)** and his followers, when they escaped from Pharaoh and his army through the *sea* that had split when Musa (as) hit the ground with his special stick.

It's also the day that Nuh's (as) ark landed on a mountain.

Ali: I remember those stories, Migo. You told me them!

Migo: That's right, my cotton ball, I did tell you them.

Musa (as) used to fast on Ashura, and then our Prophet (saw) did too, because of his love and respect for Musa (as). If you fast on Ashura, you get lots and lots of blessings and Allah forgives the wrong things you might have done. We fast one day before Ashura, or one day after Ashura, too.

A'udhoobiLLah

A'udhoobillah are very *strong* words. When you say them, you are asking for Allah's **PROTECTION** against Shaytan. It's like putting on an imaginary cloak that makes sure Shaytan can't bother you anymore. If you have the 'cloak' on, Shaytan runs away, scared. These words are your cloak! They can help you to get rid of Shaytan and any bad thoughts that might be creeping into your head.

ALi: When shall I say A'udhoobillah, Migo?

Migo : Well, saying A'udhoobillah can cool you down when you are becoming a hot head. So you should say it when you feel like you're getting angry. You should also say it when you're having thoughts which aren't good. Like if you feel jealous of someone, or you plan to do something which isn't right. And when beginning to recite Quran, so that nothing can distract you from the beautiful words you are reciting.

Ayat

An ayat is one of the verses that come together to make a surah in the Quran, like sentences in a book come together to make a whole chapter, or like bricks come together to make a wall.

Here's an example from Surah Ikhlas:
'Qul hu-wallahu ahad', is one verse, or ayat. **Each ayat is special and makes sense on its own.** In fact, the ayats in the Qur'an are each amazing words from Allah, with special meanings.

Ali: Migo, I love reading ayats from the Qur'an, till I get to the end of the surah!

Migo: Yes you do, my flower petal, and I love hearing you.

Beard

A beard is a growth of hair on a face. Beards are sunnah, which means that the Prophet (saw) had a beard. All the sahaba, the men who had the pleasure of knowing or meeting the Prophet, had beards too.

Ali: Do you have a beard, Migo?

Migo: I think I do, but it blends in with the rest of my fur so you can't tell.

Ali: Haha, OK. How does a beard make people feel?

Migo: Well, when I stroke my beard it makes me feel really smart!

Bismillah

Bismillah means, 'In Allah's name'. We should say it before we eat and it's also great to say it when starting anything at all.

It's like when you're about to climb up really high, or even jump down once you're there, it feels a lot better when you say to an adult, "Watch me!"

It feels safer, just because someone is watching. Well bismillah is like that, except it is Allah you are calling out to – and He listens every time! Imagine that! Allah watching over whatever you do to make sure it goes well - that's what bismillah is.

Ali: I say bismillah before I eat.

Migo: I say bismillah when I come home.

Ali: I say bismillah before reciting from the Qur'an.

Migo: I say bismillah before changing my clothes.

Ali: Wait, you wear clothes? Haha!

Migo: Haha! Don't be cheeky!

Ali: I say bismillah before making wudu.

Migo: I say bismillah before driving my car or riding a horse.

But guess what, Ali? I even say bismillah when I am a bit frightened to start something. Starting it in Allah's name comforts me. **And I say it before doing anything at all!**

I even say bismillah when I turn the washing machine on.

I even say bismillah when I am picking a flower.

I even say bismillah when I am building a Lego tower.

I even say bismillah when I am starting to **write**.

I even say bismillah when I am **paying** for something.

I even say bismillah when I am about to **bake** or **cook**.

I even say bismillah when I am turning my **computer on**.

I say bismillah because if I mention the **name of Allah**, Shaytan will not be able to mess with what I am doing, with his **TRICKS**. Instead, he will buzz off and whatever I am doing will be **full of blessings!**

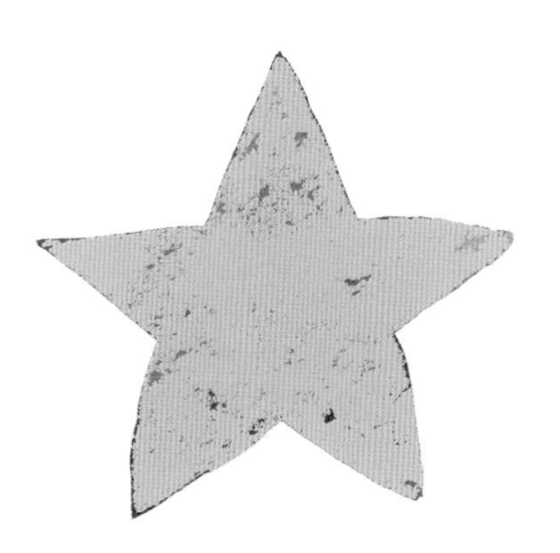

Dhikr

Dhikr means saying the name of Allah, or even thinking of Him in your mind. When you make dhikr, it is a way of worshipping Allah. Some things you can say to make dhikr are:

SubhanAllah

Alhamdulillah

Allahu Akbar

Astagfirullah

SubhanAllahi Wa bihamdihi SubhanAllah hil-adheem

It's good to have a think about the meanings of these words so that you can say the right ones at the right time and really mean it!

ALi: Like when Allah gives me ice-cream, I can say Alhamdulillah and really mean it!

Migo: Haha, exactly like that, my cookies and cream cone.

When you make dhikr, you get lots of rewards from Allah and He forgives you for doing some things you shouldn't have done.

Once, the Prophet's (saw) daughter Fatima was really tired and she asked him for a servant to help her. The Prophet (saw) knew that the words that mention Allah are more powerful than the help of a servant, so he told her to say these words:

SUBHANALLAH

33 times

ALHAMDULILLAH

33 times

ALLAHUAKBAR

34 times

You can make dhikr anytime and anywhere.

You can do it while you're laying down to sleep in your bed.

Or riding your bike.

Or even when on the swing. Allah loves it if you think of Him no matter what you are doing.

Dua

Dua is a way of **talking to Allah**, to *thank* Him and to *ask* Him for things. Allah loves to be asked, even for small things, and for Allah, no thing is too small or too big.

You should make dua all the time, **right from your heart**. You can tell Allah about some *good things* you have done and what your **TROUBLES** are. It's an **amazing and beautiful thing to be able to talk to Allah whenever we want, wherever we want and about whatever we want.** We don't need anyone else to talk to Him for us, every person in the world can ask Allah for anything, all by themselves. And Allah listens to them *all*. He is the one who has **power** over everything, so He can give you what He wants if He thinks it's best for you.

Ali: But can I still ask other people to make dua for me too?

Migo: Absolutely, and you should also make dua for others. In fact when you make dua for others, the angels make the same dua for you.

Ali: Wow!

Migo: You can make dua in English or any other language. But there are some wonderful duas in the Qur'an and some that the Prophet (saw) used to make, which you can learn from ahadith.

There are also manners that would make your dua even better if you followed them. Here are some of them:

Have belief in Allah as one, and trust in Him

Praise Allah and send blessings on the Prophet (saw)

Face the Qibla

Raise your hands

Eid

Ali: Eid is a day when we get presents and eat a lot!

Migo: Haha, my present muncher! It is, yes, but it's much more than that too!

We have two Eids in a year, and they are the days on which we celebrate our love for Allah and the rewards He has given us.

Eid-Al-Fitr comes after we have fasted for a whole month of Ramadan. We celebrate that Allah gave us the chance to do that, and to become clean and pure and forgiven.

Ali: And that we can eat in the daytime again!

Migo: Haha, cheeky monkey. Yes, why not, we should eat the foods we love on Eid. In fact, you're not even allowed to fast on Eid, so you must eat, pray, give charity and be happy!

Eid Al Adha is the second Eid in the year. It's the more special one. It means the feast of sacrifice. It comes on the **10th day of Dhul Hijjah** (see Islamic months), which is when the Muslims have finished their **Hajj** and are forgiven by Allah.

Ali: Wait, Migo. What does sacrifice mean? Do you mean sack of rice?

Migo: Haha, Ali, you silly biscuit. No, it means when you give something up, something that you really wanted or love, but you give it up for someone else.

ALi: Oh, like when you didn't get a pudding the other day, so I gave you mine, even though I really wanted it?

Migo: Yes, like that! Except, on this Eid, we make a sacrifice for Allah.

ALi: What do we sacrifice?

Migo: You sacrifice an animal, and share the meat with the poor people. You can also have some for yourself and your family. And we do this to remember that Ibrahim (as) loved Allah so much, that he would even give up his son for Allah. But Allah didn't let him. He made it so that Ibrahim (as) gave up a sheep for Him instead.

ALi: Then I want to give up a sheep this Eid too, Migo!

Migo: OK, my butter cup.

Fard

As Muslims, there are some things that we absolutely **MUST** do and there are other things that we don't have to do, but that are really good for us if we do them.

The things that we must do, are called fard.

When you are old enough, it is fard to pray your salah five times a day, to fast in Ramadan, go for Hajj (if you can) and pay your zakat. They are things that you can't choose not to do.

FARD

Five Pillars of Islam

The Five Pillars of Islam are the five **most important things you must do as a Muslim.** The Arabic word for pillars is 'arkan.' When a house is built, pillars are used to hold it up with *strength.* All the pillars are important, and if any of them are a bit wobbly, the whole house will be a bit wobbly. Just like that, every pillar of Islam is important. We must do all of them with strength so that our faith isn't wobbly.

Ali: Do you know who wants to live in a wobbly house, Migo?

Migo: Who?!

Ali: Nobody!

Migo: Hahaha. That's right. Nobody!

Strong House

The Five Pillars are:

• Shahadah: This is saying out loud that you very truly believe that there is only one God, Allah, and that Muhammad (saw) is His messenger. **"ASH-HADU ANLA ILAHA ILLA-ALLAH WA ASH-HADU ANNA MUHAMMADAN RASUL-ALLAH".**

• Salat: Doing your salah (prayers) five times a day (see Salah).

• Zakat: Giving charity to poor people (see Zakat).

• Sawm: Fasting during the month of Ramadan (see Ramadan).

• Hajj: Going on a journey to Makkah, for Allah. It is called a pilgrimage (see Hajj).

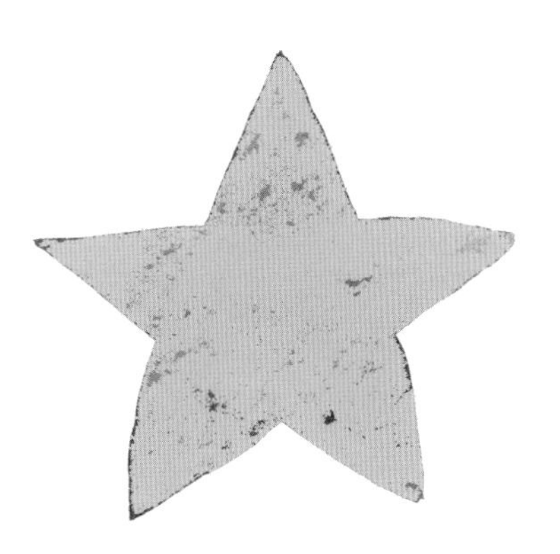

Ghusl

A ghusl is a way of cleaning yourself to make yourself pure. It can be done in the shower, or the bath, or even the ocean or a river! As long as you take away the dirt from every part of your body and make wudu.

Hadith

A hadith tells us things that the Prophet Muhammad (saw) said and did. The people who were around him, when he was alive, wrote these things down.

ALi: Why?

Migo: So that people can learn from them.
For example, imagine I made up a cake recipe and it was really good and I would bake it with you all the time. Even if I wrote down the instructions,

there might be some things that people want to **know** about it, and you could tell them, because you spent a lot of time with me, making the cake. **THEY MIGHT WANT TO KNOW WHAT HAPPENS IF THEY DROP SOME OF THE FLOUR ON THE FLOOR**, or what to do if they don't have an oven.

Now, because you are very close to me and spent a lot of time making the cake with me, people would believe you if you said that you know what to do if some of the flour falls down. But, if someone who has never met me said that they know what to do if the flour falls down, people wouldn't believe them! **Hadith are like that too. We know which hadith are strong and which ones are weak, depending on who told them.**

We use both the Qur’an and Hadith to understand how to live our lives the way that Allah wants us to.

Ali: Wow, Migo. I really like hadith, because I want to know lots and lots about what the Prophet (saw) said.

Migo: Me too, my bun with lots of sugar on top.

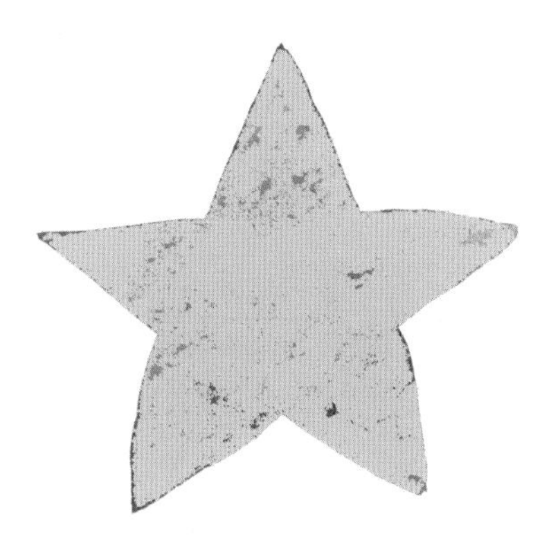

Hajj

Hajj is a journey to Makkah, for Allah. When people go on a journey to a special place, for God, it is called a pilgrimage. Hajj happens once a year. Millions of people, from all over the world, go to Makkah for it. It is one of the five pillars of Islam (see Five Pillars).

Ali: Really, Migo? ALL over the world?

Migo: Yes, my sweetest turnip, because there are Muslims in every part of the world.

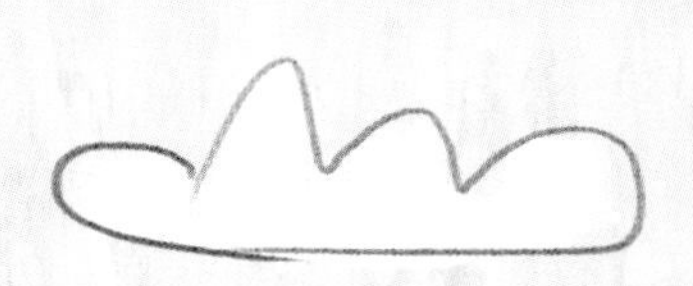

Ali: But do they all have to go, every year?

Migo: Haha, no. Every Muslim has to go at least once in their lifetime. That's if they have enough money to do it and if their body is able to do it.

People have been going to the Kaabah, in Makkah, to worship for many, many years, since **Ibrahim** (as) and his son **Ismail** (as) built it. But after a while, people had started doing it all *wrong.* They started putting *statues* inside the Kaabah and praying to those instead of Allah.

The Prophet Muhammad (saw) sorted all of that out, and made things the way that Allah really wants them. He showed people how to do Hajj properly, and we've been doing it like that ever since.

ALi: That's amazing, Migo!

Migo: Yes, it really is!

ALi: When do people do it?

Migo: The Hajj is from the 8th to the 12th of Dhul Hijjah. That's the 12th and last month of the Islamic calendar (see Islamic Calendar).

To do the Hajj, we need to go into ihram, which is a special way of behaving, which keeps us pure for the special journey.

Ali: Is it like wudu?

Migo: Hmmm, not exactly, but a little bit. You have to make wudu before praying. In that way, it's similar, because you have to go into ihram to do the Hajj or Umrah. But wudu can break and doesn't last very long, whereas you can go into ihram for days!

Ali: Sometimes wudu only lasts a few mins, for some people. Haha.

Migo: You cheeky little biscuit!

Ali: Haha, OK, tell me Migo!

Migo: For ihram, you have to get all cleaned up, and cut your nails. You are not allowed to wear perfume, or even use lotions or soaps with perfume. You put on clean clothes, then you make the intention to do the Hajj and say these special words, called the talbiya:

"Labbayk Allaahumma labbayk, labbayka laa shareeka laka labbayk. Inna al-hamd wa'l-ni'mata laka wa'l-mulk, laa shareeka lak"

This means, "Here I am in Your service, O Allah, here I am. Here I am, You have no partner, here I am. All praise and blessings are Yours, and all power. You have no partner."

For ihram, women wear their normal clothes that cover them up. But all men have to wear only two **simple white sheets.** One at the top, and one at the bottom. They have to wear sandals, which don't cover the top of the foot, and they mustn't cover their head.

When you're in ihram, you are not allowed to cut your nails or hair, or kill anything, not even a fly. **You have to be on your best behaviour.**

Ali: And then what do the people do for Hajj? How long does it take?

Migo: It takes days. On the first day of Hajj, the pilgrims (people who are doing Hajj) go from Makkah to Mina. Mina is another little town. Some people walk there and some people go by car or coach. Can you imagine? There are millions of people, all there for Allah, making their way to Mina. They all recite the talbiya, with a love for Allah in their hearts. People of all colours, shapes and sizes go. It's quite a beautiful feeling to be part of it.

Then they stay the whole day and night in Mina. There are special white tents that all the pilgrims sleep in.

Ali: Wow, I love camping!

Migo: Yes, it's a bit like camping, but a lot more special!

The next day is called the **DAY OF ARAFAH**.

It's on the 9th of Dhul-Hijjah. If anyone from your family or friends has gone for the wonderful journey of Hajj, on this day after Fajr Salah, they will be **marching by foot or driving in cars and buses to a place called Arafah.** There will be millions of people all going to the same place, at the same time, **peacefully**, and all of them will be saying to Allah: "Here I am in Your service, O Allah, here I am. Here I am, You have no partner, here I am. All praise and blessings are Yours, and all power, You have no partner."

Ali: That's the talbiya!

Migo: Perfect, you remember!

When they get to Arafah they listen to a special talk at Dhuhr time, and pray. They spend the whole day praying, reading Qur'an and making dua. Allah is so pleased with the people, His mercy comes down to the lowest heaven, and He says: "Look at My servants. They have come from far and near, with hair all messy and faces covered with dust, to seek My mercy..."

In Arafah there is a mountain called Mount Arafat or the Mount of Mercy. Prophet Muhammad (saw) stood on it to give a talk to his people during Hajj.

Even if you're not on Hajj, this day is special! We should fast on the day of Arafah because if we do, insha'Allah our sins for the last year and the one to come will be forgiven. We should also carry on reciting Takbir, Tahmid, Tahleel and Tasbih (see Takbir, Tahmid, Tahleel and Tasbih).

The people who are making Hajj must stay in Arafah on this day, only then will their Hajj be complete. At sunset, people start to leave Arafah and they go to a place called **MUZDALIFAH** to pray Maghrib and Isha and rest for the night, under the stars, without a tent.

Ali: Woah, Migo. Under the stars?!

Migo: Yes indeed, my apple and blueberry crumble. It's quite beautiful.

The next day is the 10th of Dhul-Hijjah, which is **EID DAY** for people who aren't doing hajj. But for the pilgrims, it isn't Eid, they have other things to do! In the morning, they collect pebbles from the ground and head back to Mina. In Mina, there is a place which is a symbol of Shaytan. *It's not really him,* it's a stone pillar, but part of Hajj is to remember any bad things that he might have made you do, and **throw seven pebbles at the pillar**. Next, they sacrifice an animal *for Allah* and give the meat to poor people to cook and enjoy. After that, they can come out of **Ihram,** by cutting a bit of their hair if they are women, or shaving their hair if they are a boy or man.

Then people go back to Makkah to do the tawaaf around the Kaaba, and the sa'ay, like you do for Umrah (see Umrah). For the next two days, back in Mina, the pilgrims throw stones at the Jamaraat again, but this time, at two more stone pillars that are symbols of Shaytan. After that, they can go back to Makkah and stay there for as long or little as they like. Before leaving Makkah, the pilgrims do a 'goodbye' tawaaf around the Kaaba; thinking about their whole Hajj and how it made them feel; how it changed them and how lucky they were that Allah chose them to come for Hajj.

HaLaL

When we say something is halal, we mean that it is allowed. It is something that Allah has made OK for us to do or eat. The opposite of halal is haram (see haram).

Before you eat something,

you should make sure that it is halal.

You can do that by

looking at the ingredients

or asking an adult.

Rice
Rice
Rice

Animals can be made halal for us to eat, but there are special **rules** to follow to do that. When the animal is made halal, **Allah's name** is said and it is done in a way that is best for it.

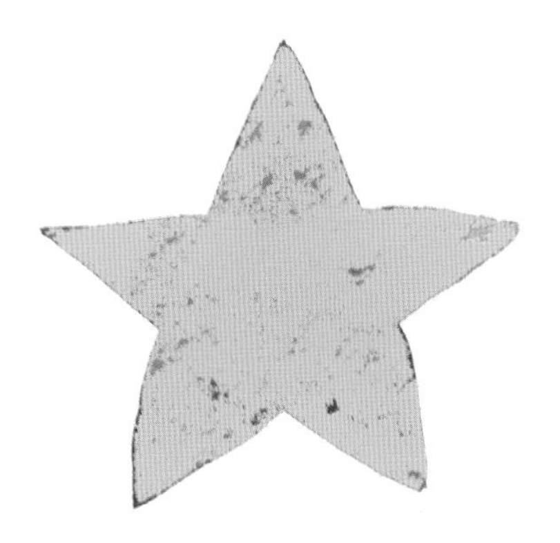

Haram

Haram means *not allowed* at all, because Allah has said so. It could be a food or even an action. When you know that something is haram, you should stay away from it, because it's not good for you at all.

Some things are haram **all the time.** And some things can be made halal. It's *always* haram to eat any part of a pig, but you can make a chicken, a cow, a goat, and some other animals halal.

Some **actions**, or things that people *do*, can be haram too, because Allah has told us exactly how to behave and live our lives. For example, stealing is haram.

These days, when people say hijab, they are talking about the covering of a lady's hair with a scarf. That means the word hijab is used to mean headscarf. But actually, **hijab is a way of acting and dressing for men and women**, that Allah has told us about. It's about the way you **behave** and also about wearing the right clothes to **cover** up the parts of us that Allah said to cover.

Hijrah

Hijrah means to move from one place to another place, to live, usually because the new place will be safer or better.

In Islam, when we say Hijrah, we are normally talking about the **amazing move that the Prophet (saw) made from Makkah to Madinah**, on which he had a very adventurous journey.

In those days, Makkah was ruled by a powerful tribe of people, called the Quraish. Everybody knew Muhammad (saw) very well. They knew he never, ever told lies and that he was kind, generous and good. But when he became a prophet and started telling people about Allah, the Quraish were cross. They didn't like that at all.

They wanted to carry on praying to the **statues** that they had made and put inside the Kaaba, and all around it. They liked how much *money* they were making from all the visitors, too. So they decided that they would not believe the Prophet (saw) and they would make things for him and any other Muslims very difficult.

They made it unbearable and very dangerous for the Prophet (saw) and his companions to live in Makkah. That's why the Prophet (saw) chose to move to a city where there were nice people who wanted to learn about Islam. That place was called **YATHRIB** and is now called **MADINAH**.

So, ever so secretly, the *Muslims started to move to Madinah.* The Prophet (saw) and some of his companions stayed behind until the time was right to go. But, in that time, the Quraish got even nastier. They made a plan to kill the Prophet (saw)! They thought they were very clever, but *nobody is smarter than Allah.* Allah knew what was going on, and He **saved** His prophet (saw).

That night, Ali (ra) **bravely** slept in the Prophet's (saw) bed instead of him. The Quraish were waiting outside, to attack when the Prophet (saw) gets up and leaves the house. In the meantime, **the Prophet and his best friend, Abu Bakr (ra) quickly escaped on camels.** When the people saw that Ali came out of the house instead of the Prophet (saw), they were surprised and very angry that their plan to kill him had failed. So they went after him - lots of men, trying to find and catch the Prophet (saw).

The Prophet (saw) and Abu Bakr (ra) hid inside a cave. Abu Bakr (ra) was a very brave friend, who worried about the Prophet (saw) a lot! While they were in the cave, he let a scorpion bite him, so that it wouldn't bite the Prophet (saw) and wake him up and cause him pain.

Some men almost found them! They came right up to the cave, but they saw that a spider had made its web across the cave and a bird had laid its eggs there. Because of that, they decided there was no way that anyone could be in there. When the men were outside the cave, Abu Bakr (ra) told the Prophet (saw) that he was *scared*. But the Prophet (saw) told him **not to worry, because even though they were only two people, Allah was the third. The Most Powerful was with them, protecting them.**

After that, they carried on their tiring and long journey on *camels* to Madinah. When they arrived, a crowd of men, women and children welcomed him. **THEY SANG SONGS BECAUSE THEY WERE SO VERY HAPPY!**

They all wanted the Prophet (saw) to come and stay at their house. Obviously, he couldn't choose, so to be fair, the Prophet (saw) said that he will stay where the camel stops. And just like that, **with Allah's help**, the camel decided.

The hijrah is so important, that the Islamic calendar starts from when it happened. The Prophet (saw) spent a lot of time living in Madinah. He **loved** everything about it. His body is buried there, and lots of people go there to say *salaam* to him and spend time in the place that the Prophet (saw) loved so much.

30
رَجَب
1
شعبان

Holy Books

The Qur'an is a holy book, which was sent down to the Prophet Muhammad (saw). There are other holy books too;

the Bible, (Injil) Torah (Tawrat) and Psalms, (Zabur)

which were sent to other prophets and messengers. The people who believed in Allah in the times of those holy books, followed those books like we follow the Qur'an. The other holy books have all been changed now, but we as Muslims must believe that they were sent to the prophets before.

The Qur'an is the only book sent by Allah that we know for sure is correct (see Qur'an).

Sent to
Esa (as)
BiBLE
Sent to
Musa (as)
Torah
Psalms
Sent to
Muhammad (saw)
Quran
Sent to
Dawud (as)

Iftar

Iftar is the food that we eat when we break our fast.

The feeling that you get at iftar, when you break your fast, is amazing. There's no feeling like it! And just like everything good and wonderful, it is from Allah.

The Prophet (saw) used to break his fast with fresh dates, if he could find them, and if he couldn’t, he would eat dried dates to break his fast. He would also drink water, which is very important.

Ali: Is that all, Migo? Some people eat a whole table of food and they don't stop eating till they fall asleep!

Migo: Haha, yes , that's true, my ball of peanuts, but it is not right. Allah has given us our bodies, and we should take care of them. Eating that much food at iftar, and the wrong kind of food is very bad for our bodies. Fasting should teach us that we can just eat small bits and that's enough for us.

z z Z Z Z

Ihsan

Ah, Ihsan. It's such a beautiful thing. It is being excellent; it is perfection; it is beauty. It is wanting to do your absolute best...

It is excellent manners and character. It is love. It is doing things that you might not even like doing, with all your strength – all for Allah...

All because you know, that at every moment in time, Allah is watching you. Allah is with you. It's as if you can see Him. Obviously, you can't, but you behave in a way as if you can, because He can see you.

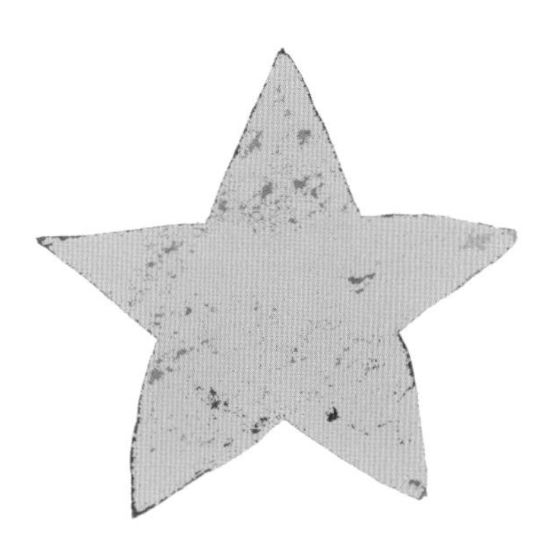

Imaan

Imaan is what is inside your heart that tells you that Allah is there. It is the feeling that tells you that *there is only one God*, who is Allah and that Allah is with you. If you have imaan, you believe in Allah and you are completely sure about it, with no doubts! You also believe in the other parts of faith (see Aqeedah).

ALi: How do you know when you have imaan, Migo? Can you see it?

Migo: No, no, my banana chip! But you can feel it. Sometimes it is big and strong and sometimes it gets smaller. You just have to take care of it, to make sure it always stays with you.

Ali: How can I take care of it?

Migo: There are lots of ways! You should always remember Allah by thinking of Him and the amazing blessings around us because of Him. You should pray and recite Qur'an. You should make dhikr (see dhikr) and do lots of good deeds. And you should talk to Allah all the time. Makes lots of dua and trust in Him.

Ali: Because He's the best!

Migo: He sure is!

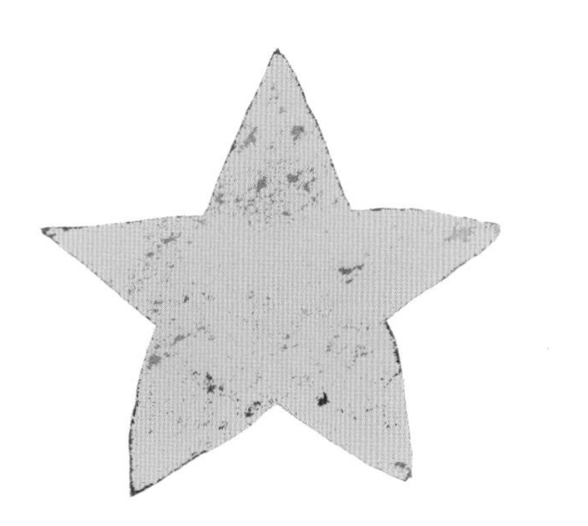

Imam

An imam is a leader. He is a leader of prayers, usually in the mosque and a leader in the community: for example, a certain area where people live. People can go to the imam, if they have a question about Islam, and he can help them. He also gives the Khutba on Jum'uah (see Khutba).

ALi: Migo, when I lead the prayer at home, am I an imam?

Migo: Yes, you certainly are! When people pray together in Salat-Al-Jama'ah, the leader of the prayer is still called the imam.

ALi: Wow, Migo, that is so cool!

In-sha-ALLah

In-sha-Allah means, 'If Allah wills,' or in other words, **if Allah wants it to happen**. We say this because we know that nothing can happen unless Allah wants it to. **No matter how much we want something to happen, or how much we try, it cannot happen unless Allah chooses for it to happen.**

ALi: I am going to visit my friend, in-sha-Allah.

Migo: Very good! I am going to eat all of this apple pie in-sha-Allah.

ALi: Haha, Migo, you just finished a whole pie!

Migo: Well I'm hungry again! I'm a bear!

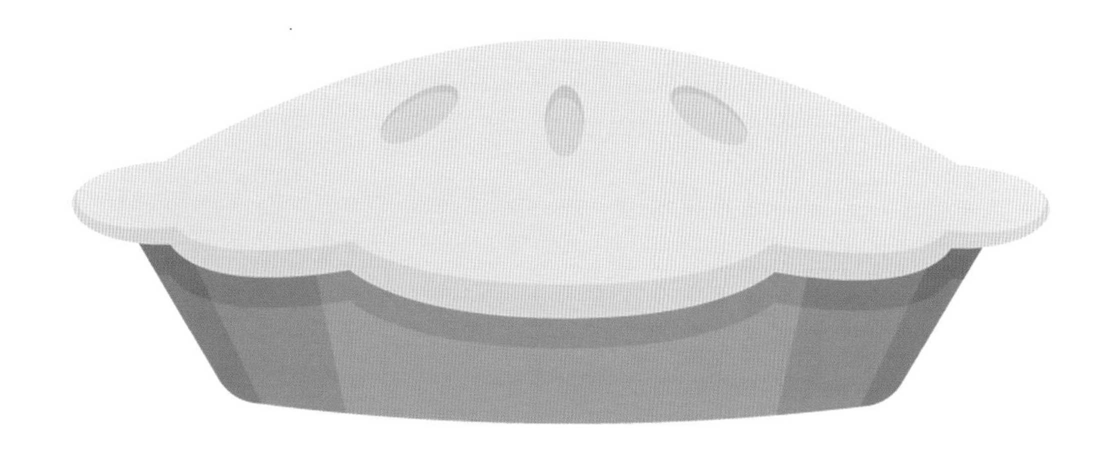

Iqama

Iqama is the call just before the jam'at prayer starts (that's when everybody prays together). It sounds quite the same as the adhaan. When you hear the iqama, you **stand up** and **get in position** to pray.

Islamic Months

In Islam, we follow a lunar calendar. That's a calendar that depends on the moon (see Moon). There are twelve Islamic months. Four of those are **sacred.** They are in green. They are extra special, so it is even better to do good deeds in those months and even worse to do bad things.

1. Muharram

2. Safar

3. Rabi' al-Awwal

4. Rabi' ath-thani

5. Jamada al-Ula

6. Jamada al-akhira

7. Rajab

8. Sha'ban

9. Shahr al-Ramadan

10. Shawwal

11. Dhu al-Qa'da

12. Dhu al-Hijjah

Israa' and Mi'raj

The Israa' was a journey that the Prophet (saw) made, one night, in the month of Rajab. He went from the Kaaba in Makkah to the **holy mosque** in Jerusalem, called **Al-Aqsa.** Unlike any journey that we make, this journey was a miracle, because he got there very, very fast on a special kind of horse with wings, called the Buraq! The Buraq is named after **lightning**, so you can imagine how fast he must be!

The angel Jibreel came to take the Prophet (saw) on this journey. They went to Madinah and prayed there and they also went to Mount Sinai, which is where Allah spoke to Musa (as) and then they went to Jerusalem. In the holy mosque there, all of the prophets met Prophet Muhammad (saw) and prayed behind him.

Then the Prophet (saw) went up through the heavens, all the way to the highest heaven until he was close to Allah. That part of the journey is called the Mi'raj.

During the Mi'raj the Prophet (saw) was given the gift of salah for us. At first, Allah had asked for us to pray 50 times in the day. Prophet Musa (as) warned Prophet Muhammad (saw) that that would be too much for us, and that we wouldn't be able to do it. He said to ask Allah to make it less. So our prophet asked Allah to make it less. Eventually, Allah made it so that we have to pray 5 times in the day.

After that, angel Jibreel took him back to the Kaaba in Makkah. When the Prophet (saw) told people the next day, many of them didn't *believe* him. But he had seen some travellers along the way back, which would be too far away to see otherwise. He described them to the people and when they showed up a few days later, people were **astonished** to see that he was right about them and then they believed him.

Jannah

Jannah is the place where in-sha-Allah, we will live forever after this life on Earth. **In English, people call it heaven.**

It's the most *wonderful* and *beautiful* place ever, and Allah made it. In Jannah there are gardens with pretty rivers flowing through. Not the kind of gardens we have here, but the most beautiful ones, with palaces to live in. You can't even imagine what they look like. In fact Jannah is so special that we can't imagine it at all. That's why there is no picture of it here. **In Jannah you will have whatever you want or wish for. You won't feel sleepy, or hungry, or angry, or any of the ways you feel here. And you will be with your family.**

Jahannam is a place that is the opposite of Jannah. It is only for people who keep doing evil, terrible things, without even being sorry for them - like the Shaytan and his followers.

Jazak-Allah-Khair

This means, 'May Allah give you a good reward,' which is a much better way of saying thank you than just saying thank you! When you say jazak-Allah-Khair, to a person, you're making a dua for them, asking Allah to give a good reward to them. That reward will be a most wonderful gift, because it's from Allah, so it's better than anything you can say or give to show that you are grateful to them.

Ali: Jazak-Allah-khair for making my sandwich, Migo.

Migo: Wa antum fa-jazakumullahu-khayran!

Ali: What does that mean?

Migo: It means, 'And to you. May Allah reward you with goodness.'

Ali: This is so nice! I get a reward from Allah just for thanking you!

Migo: Indeed, my candyfloss cloud. Islam is beautiful like that.

Jum'uah

Jum'uah is the Arabic word for Friday. It's a special day - Allah loves it a lot! It's like having a little Eid, every week. That's because, on this day, there are many blessings to be found.

There is a special prayer in the mosque on Jum'uah, at Dhuhr time. A khutba (see khutba), which is a special talk, is given by the imam (see imam) of the mosque.

On Jum’uah, everyone should clean themselves and put on nice, clean clothes and perfume and use a miswaak (see miswaak).

ALi: So can I wear dirty clothes all the other days, Migo?

Migo: Haha, no cheeky cheeks, you cannot! It's just that on Jum'uah, you can make an extra effort. On Jum'uah, we read Surah Kahf from the Qur'an. That's because, if you do, there will be a light in your life from that Jum'uah to the next!

Ali: Wow, amazing! And guess what, Migo? I know something about Jum'uah too...

Migo: Ah, what is it you clever little pear-drop?

Ali: Allah made Adam (as) on Jum'uah!

Migo: Yes, He did. That really is clever of you!

On Jum'uah, we should say lots of salawat (peace and blessings) to the Prophet (saw).

Another amazing thing about Jum'uah is that the angels stand at the entrance of a masjid where Jum'uah Salah is about to happen, and write down the names of the people coming, until the khutbah begins.

Ali: Wow, Jum'uah is amazing, Migo.

Migo: It is. And on Jum'uah, you should make lots of duas all day, because there is one hour in that day in which your dua will definitely be accepted.

Ali: I will, Migo! in-sha-Allah, I will.

Kaaba

The Kaaba is Allah's house. It is a cube shaped building in Makkah, and when we pray, we all face towards the Kaaba. That's called the **Qibla**. We also go to it to do Umrah and Hajj (see Umrah and Hajj). The *Kaaba was first made by Adam (as)* and then made again by **IBRAHIM (AS) AND HIS SON ISMAIL (AS)**.

ALi: I know! I know the story from when you told me before!

Migo: Yes you do, my bubble on a rainy day!

The Kaaba is still there today, but people did have to keep fixing it and building it again. It has a beautiful black cloth to cover it.

Before the Prophet's (saw) time, silly people had started to put statues inside the Kaaba to pray to them and more silly people used to come from all around to pray to the statues. **When the Prophet (saw) was in control of Makkah, he broke all of those statues and everyone started using the Kaaba like it is supposed to be used.**

When you go for Umrah and Hajj, you do tawaaf around the Kaaba, which is a way of worshipping Allah, by walking around the Kaaba (see Umrah and Hajj).

There is a Black stone on the Kaaba, which has been sent down by Allah, from heaven! It used to be white! In Prophet Muhammad's (saw) story, you will remember that all the tribes were fighting about how to put it back on. If you can touch the black stone, it is very good.

Ali: Migo, remember when we tried to touch the black stone and I was on your shoulders and then that man pushed you so hard and I almost fell off?

Migo: Yes, oh dear. It is very hard to touch it, because these days there are so many people around the Kaaba, who are trying to touch it. It can get a bit crazy, and yes, people push each other, but there is really no point of touching it if you have to hurt someone to do it, or if you behave in a rude way.

Ali: So Migo, when we go for Umrah and Hajj, are we praying to the Kaaba?

Migo: No, no, my sweet. We are praying to Allah and only Allah.

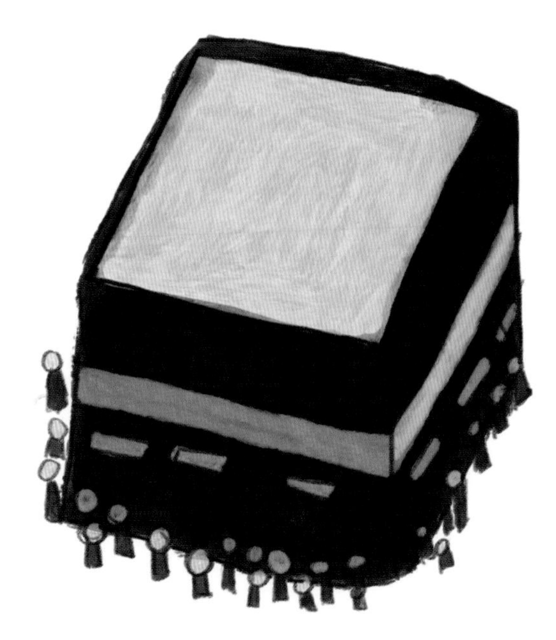

Khutbah

Khutba is the Arabic word for giving a speech, or talk, to do with things about Islam.

On Jum'uah (see Jum'uah) a khutba is given at Dhuhr time instead of 2 units of prayer. So **the Khutba is just as important as the Dhuhr salah on Jum'uah**, and just as you wouldn't talk or mess about while you are praying your salah, you shouldn't talk during the khutba.

Actually, if you get to the mosque on time for the khutba, and sit *quietly* and listen to every word, you will have lots and lots of **rewards** from Allah and Allah will let you off for any not so good

things you might have done during the week...

Ali: Haha, Migo, why are you looking at me like that? Do you know what I did?

Migo: Ali, I always know what you did. I know you better than you know the cookie jar!

Laylatul Qadr

Laylatul Qadr is a night in the last ten days of Ramadan, that is better than a thousand months. If we worship Allah on this night, it counts for us worshipping him for 83 years.

On Laylatul Qadr, the angels come down to Earth. There are so many of them, that the whole of the Earth is covered. There are more angels here that night than there are grains of sand, and as you know, there are a LOT of grains of sand.

Ali: Migo, what happens on Laylatul Qadr?
Migo: Well, my magical star, Allah talks about you to the angels! He tells them everything that is

going to happen to you over the year.

ALi: Wow! He talks about me? Why does He tell the angels what's going to happen to me?

Migo: Because, angels have different jobs to do, so they need to know what's happening. Maybe an angel has to stop something from falling on you when you're walking down the road.

ALi: Wow, because Allah didn't want it to hit me! So what should we do on this special night, Migo?

Migo: You should try to stay awake as long as you can, and make dua, pray salah, do dhikr, give charity, recite Qur'an and any other good deeds you can think of.

ALi: Like an angel?

Migo: Haha, yes, be as angelic as possible!

Madinah

Madinah is the city that the Prophet (saw) moved to when he left Makkah. The Prophet (saw) loved Madinah very, very much.

Madinah
the city of
the prophet

He loved its **people**, its **land**, its **sand** and its **fruits**. It was where the first mosque was built and it was where the Prophet (saw) passed away.

The city used to be called Yathrib before. And now it is known as **MADINAH** and also **MADINAHTUN NABI** – The City of the Prophet. It's also known as **MUNAWARAH**, which means, 'filled with light', because when the Prophet (saw) went to Madinah, the people said that it felt that the city was lit up, and when he passed away, it felt that it was dark again.

The people of Madinah were very kind. They were called the Ansar (helpers). They loved the Prophet (saw) more than they loved *themselves*. When things were very hard for the Prophet (saw) and the other Muslims in Makkah, the people of Madinah welcomed them all to come and live there and teach them about Islam.

These days, the mosque of the Prophet (saw) is still there. Millions of people visit it when they go for Umrah and Hajj, to say salaam to the Prophet (saw), who is buried there. Abu Bakr (ra) and Omar (ra) are buried there too. There is also a very special place inside that mosque, called the Rawdat-ul Jannah (garden of paradise).

Maa-sha-ALLah

When you see something *wonderful*, *beautiful*, or *amazing*, you say Maa-sha-Allah because you are remembering that **Allah made it that way.**

For example, if you make a really nice piece of art, or do some fantastic homework, you should say Maa-sha-Allah.

Masjid

A masjid is a building made for people to come to pray to Allah and to get together and be there for each other. The English name for it, is mosque.

A Mu'adhin (see Mu'adhin) calls the adhan five times a day, at the masjid, and people who live around that masjid, or are just passing by, come in to pray.

An Imam (see Imam) leads the prayer and all the men and women and children pray behind him. The masjid should be a place of comfort for a Muslim and if you love the masjid, Allah loves you!

The Prophet (saw) said that the best places on Earth are the masjids. There are lots and lots of rewards from Allah, for people who build masjids, even teeny tiny ones. That means people who do anything to help towards making the masjid. It could be laying the bricks or donating money, or anything that helps make a new masjid. Allah gives those people houses in paradise (see Jannah). We are supposed to keep our masjids pure and clean.

The masjid is not only a place to go for **salah** (see salah), it is a place where you can **learn**, recite the **Qur'an**, or make **dhikr** and **du'a**. You can also meet your **friends and family** at the masjid and have a chin wag, or plan important projects.

Ali: What's a chin wag, Migo?
Migo: It's when you're chatting away so much that it looks like your chin is wagging.

ALi: Haha, that's so funny, Migo. But I get told off for chatting in the masjid.

Migo: Well, you're not supposed to chat when the prayer or khutba (see Khutba) is going on, but later, you can. It's a great place to see your friends, my little fluff of cloud.

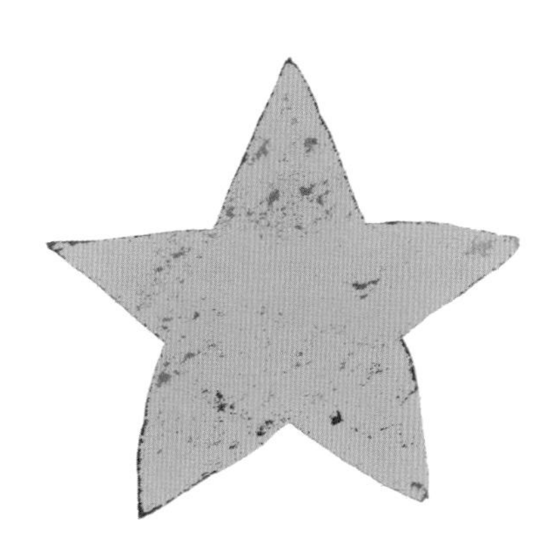

Miswaak

A miswaak is a toothbrush from a tree.

Ali: What? For bears?

Migo: Hahaha, no, for humans! The Prophet (saw) used to clean his teeth with one, and the other prophets did too! It's basically a twig from a peelu tree, or an olive tree, or a walnut tree.

Ali: Why would they brush their teeth with a twig, Migo!?

Migo: Well, my little tree climber, because the miswaak is loved by Allah and it's a very good toothbrush, with the very best toothpaste all built-in. If you use a miswaak before your prayers, you get 70 times more reward!

There's also a lot that it can do for your teeth and gums. It fights bacteria and gum disease and gets rid of bad breath.

Ali: I'm going to get one!

Migo: That's the best idea, ever!

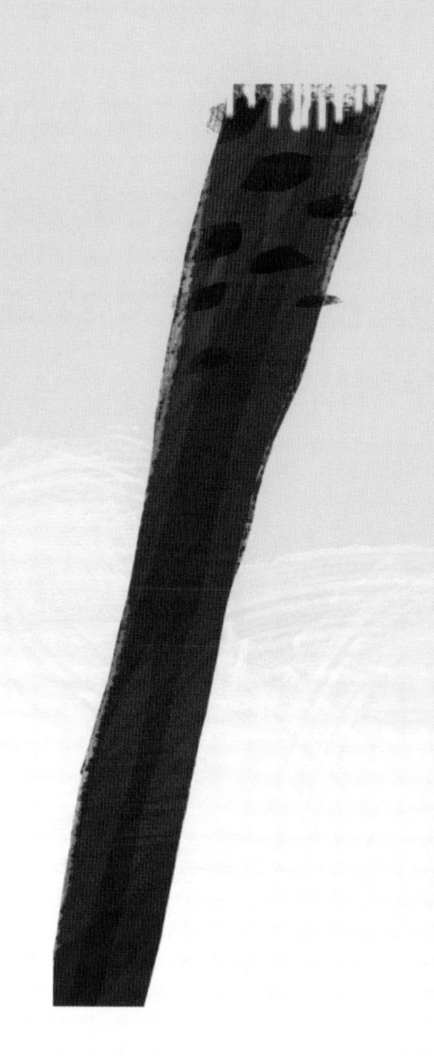

Moon

In Islam, we use the moon to tell us when each month of the year **FINISHES** and a *new* one begins (see Islamic months). Just like we use the sun to tell us what time of the day it is and when to pray.
In the past, some people used to pray to the sun and the moon. That is not right and we don't do that, we just use it like a clock and a calendar.

One month in Islam is the time it takes from one new moon to the next. You can tell if there is a new moon by looking at it.

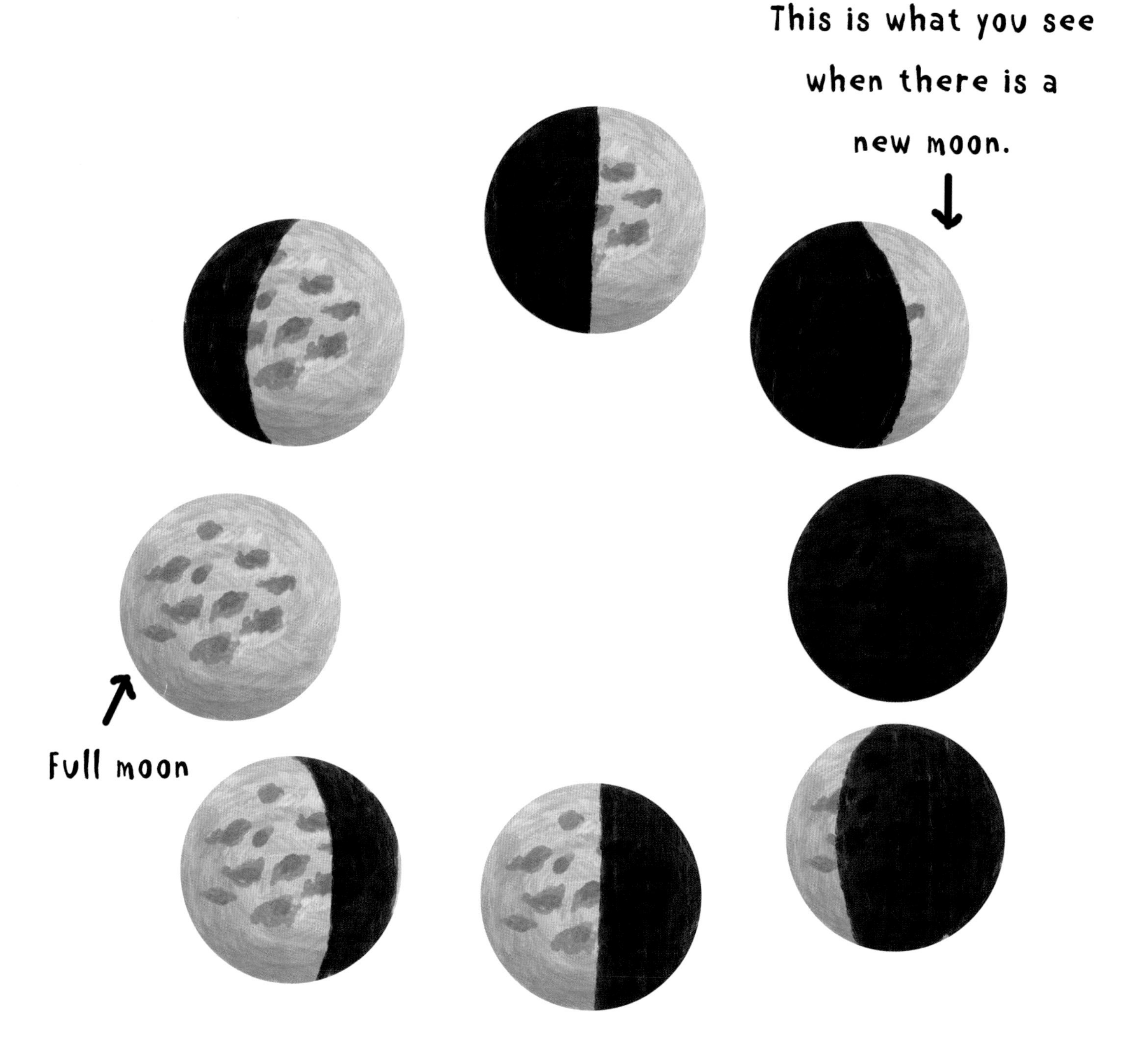

Allah mentions the moon many times in the **QUR'AN** and there is even a whole surah named after the moon, called **Surah Al-Qamar**. One of the amazing *miracles* that the Prophet (saw) showed people, was the moon splitting into two!

The new Islamic month begins when we can see a new moon.

ALi: Migo, I know about this, because when Ramadan is coming, we always look for the moon to see if it's started and then we look for the moon to see if it is Eid or not!
Migo: Yes! It's a lot of fun and we get very excited about doing that, don't we?
ALi: Yes, I love doing it Migo. Especially if we find out that it's Eid!

Mu'adhin

The Mu'adhin is the person that gives the adhaan (see Adhaan).

The job of the mu'adhin is very important. Allah gives lots of reward for doing it.

"ALLahu-Akbar,
ALLahu-Akbar..."

Prayer Mat

A prayer mat, or sajada in Arabic, is a piece of cloth that we lay on the ground, when praying. We use it to make sure that the place where we are praying, is *clean*. During the prayer, we make sujood (see Sujood), so our faces are touching the ground and also our knees, legs and hands. That's why it's nice to be sure that the place where we are doing this, is clean. Also, Allah has told us to make sure that there is nothing impure where we are praying so if we use a prayer mat, we can be happy and certain that there isn't.

You don't absolutely have to use a prayer mat when you pray. If you know that the area where you are praying is clean, you can just pray there without an extra mat.

Some people have rooms in their houses where nobody ever takes shoes or dirty things. They can pray there without using a mat.

Ali: Migo, once I saw a man in a park using a carrier bag to pray on. Why did he do that?

Migo: Ah! He was using the carrier bag as a prayer mat. You can use anything that is clean, really. We just use lovely mats and carpets because we can and because praying is such a beautiful thing that we should be clean, neat and lovely when we pray. But if you need to pray and you don't have a prayer mat, you can just lay down anything that is clean.

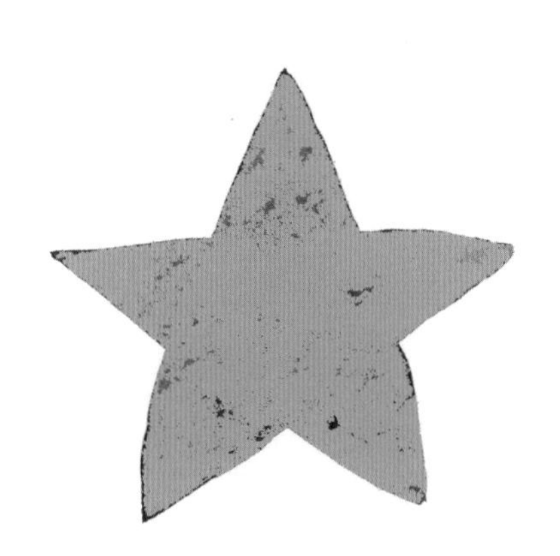

Prophets and messengers

Ali: We know all about those, don't we, Migo?!

Migo: Yes, from the time that I told you all of the exciting stories of the prophets!

Prophets and messengers have a very special job, of telling people about Allah. That there is only one Allah, and that we should worship Him. They are chosen by Allah to do that. As Muslims, we must believe in all the prophets. It is part of our faith (see Aqeedah).

There were hundreds of **PROPHETS** and **MESSENGERS**. The **Qur'an** tells us that Allah told us about some of them and didn't tell us about some of the others. All the different types of people, all through the years were sent prophets, who spoke their language.

Ali: What's the difference between prophets and messengers?

Migo: Messengers are the ones who bring the people something new and different, like a new book. For example, Esa (as) was a messenger. He was given the Bible, and the people followed that until another messenger, Muhammad (saw) was given the Qur'an to teach to people. There are lots of prophets after a messenger has brought a book to follow, to keep teaching people to follow it. But then, when a new book comes, it is given to a prophet who is also a messenger. The prophets stopped coming after the Prophet (saw), because Allah said he is the last, that's why now it's our job as Muslims to carry on telling people about Allah.

Ali: Wait, Migo! Does that mean that messengers are prophets too? But some prophets aren't messengers?

Migo: Exactly! Wow, you had to be very smart to figure that one out!

Qibla

The Qibla, is the direction we must pray in, when we do our salah. When we face the Qibla, for our prayers, we are facing the direction of the Kaaba, which means, if we were able to walk in a straight line, from where we are standing, we would eventually reach the Kaaba.

Ali: Woah! But that would take ages, Migo.
Migo: Yes, it definitely would, all the way from here, but that's where we would end up.

It's a beautiful thing, because whenever a Muslim prays, wherever they are praying, they all face the same way, which is the way that Allah chose.

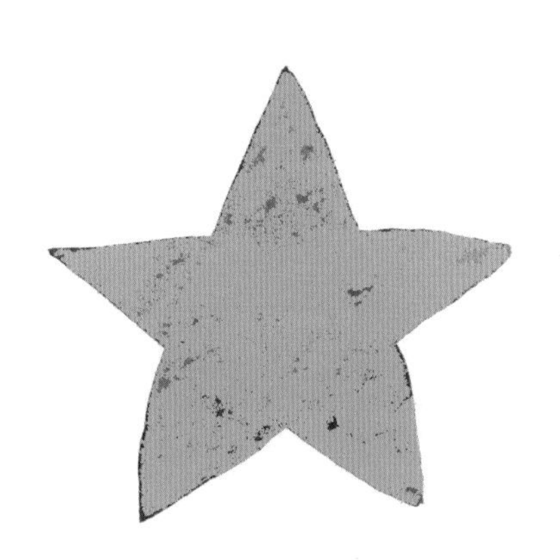

Qiyam

Qiyam is staying up at night, to pray to Allah, when most people are sleeping.

The word qiyam means 'standing.' Sometimes, people call it Qiyam-al-Layl, which means 'standing in the night.'

You don't always have to stand, because for qiyam, you can read Qur'an and remember Allah with dhikr (see Dhikr).

Ali: Migo, we did lots of qiyam in the last ten nights of Ramadan!

Migo: Yes indeed, my fluff cloud, we did. That's because, there is lots of reward for doing that, and we were hoping to catch Laylatul Qadr (see Laylatul Qadr).

Ali: Why don't we do qiyam every night?

Migo: Because it's not like the fard prayers, that everyone must do. It's your choice if you want to or not, but obviously Allah loves it and it makes us closer to Him and helps us to do good deeds. Let's stay up tonight, Ali.

Ali: To have jelly beans and fizzy cola?

Migo: No, cheeky banana, for qiyam!

Ali: Haha, Migo I know, I'm just joking. Let's do it!

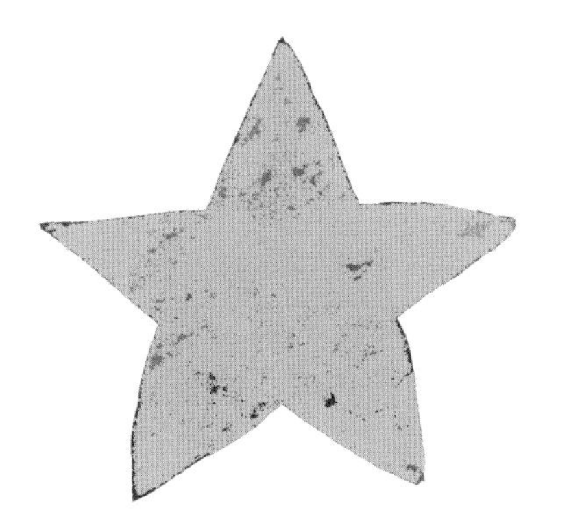

Quraish

The Quraish was a tribe, which is a group of people, who lived in Makkah in the Prophet's (saw) time. They controlled Makkah and the Kaaba. The Prophet (saw) was also a member of the Quraish tribe, and the four caliphs were also from the Quraish. There is a surah in the Qur'an called Surah Quraish, because it was sent down for them.

At first, the Quraish were against the Prophet (saw) and caused many problems for him and the other people who chose Islam, but later, the Quraish became Muslim too.

Ali: Were there lots of different tribes in Makkah in those days, Migo?
Migo: Yes, my sunset on a sunny day, there were other tribes too, but the Quraish was the strongest and most important one.

Qur'an

The Qur'an is our holy book. It was given to the Prophet Muhammad (saw) to teach us how we should live our lives.

ALi: I **love** the Qur'an, Migo. I love reading it out loud!

Migo: Yes, my sweet voiced blueberry, that's called reciting. You should do it in your most beautiful voice.

The meaning of the word Qur'an is that it is **recited all the time, very often.** And this is true, in fact, millions of people around the world have even **memorised** the Qur'an, so they know it all by heart!

We believe that the Qur'an is the **actual speech of Allah.**

That means the words in the Qur'an were actually said to the Prophet (saw) through angel Jibreel. It was amazing when the words came down, because they were so *beautiful* and had so much meaning in them.

The Qur'an is *perfect*. No human can match its perfectness. In the times that the Qur'an was revealed, people were very proud of their rhyming and poetry skills. They were excellent at it. But when they were challenged to try to write something similar to the beautiful words of the Qur'an, **they just couldn't.**

Ramadan

Ramadan is one of the months in the Islamic calendar. You might have already realised that it is a very special month, during which Muslims fast, because it is one of the five pillars of Islam. Ramadan is special, because it was the month that the Qur'an was first sent down to the Prophet (saw). During this month, Allah gives us seventy times more reward for praying, than we get in other months. Also, the Shaytaan is locked up for the whole month of Ramadan,
and the doors of heaven are open.

During this month, we try to become better people, by doing more good deeds, especially charity, and by being closer to Allah and feeling Him watching us all the time.

Ali: That's why I can't hide in my cupboard and eat when I'm fasting, because Allah still knows!

Migo: Haha, yes of course! Allah knows everything, even if we hide.

There are also special prayers in Ramadan, called Taraweeh. They are done with Isha Salah. In the mosque, during these special prayers, the Imam goes through the **whole Qur'an** from beginning to end, over the 29 or 30 days of Ramadan. Taraweeh is done two units at a time and can be done at home too.

Ali: And there is Laylatul Qadr!

Migo: Haha, yes my bouncy marshmallow, there's Laylatul Qadr, the Night of Power.

Ali: It's in the last ten nights of Ramadan, but we don't know when, so we have to try to find it!

Migo: Haha, yes but not like I find you in hide and seek, we just try our best to do qiyam on those nights.

Ramadan
St Su Mo Tu We Fri
1 2 3 4 5 6
7 8 9 10 11 12
13 14 15 16 17 18
19 20 21 22 23 24
25 26 27 28 29 30

There are some words that you hear a lot in Ramadan, here's what they all mean:

Fasting/sawm: In Islam, this means not eating anything at all during daylight hours and being on your best behaviour!

Suhoor: The meal that is eaten at that exciting and dark time, just before Fajr. It gives you blessings and energy to last through the day when you're fasting.

Iftar: This is the meal that we eat when we open our fast at sunset, which is maghrib time.

Qiyam: spending some of the night worshipping Allah.

Zakat: Making all of your money, or wealth, pure and clean by giving some of it to poor people.

Of course, right after the month of Ramadan, comes Eid!

ALi: I know which Eid, Migo! It's Eid-ul-Fitr, the one when I get the most presents.

Migo: Haha, yes, Ali, you absolutely do!

Ruku

Ruku is one of the actions we do in our salah (prayer). It's when we bend down and put our hands on our knees and say:

'Subhaana Rabbi Al Adheem'
'Glory be to my Lord, The Greatest!'

You bow to Allah, because He is glorious and the only one who you would ever bow to. You feel humble in front of Him.

Sadaqa

Sadaqa is giving away something of yours, to help someone else who needs it, just because you want to. It could be money, but it doesn't have to be. You can give your time to help people or you could even give something as small as half a date. Even smiling is a sadaqa!

Allah *loves* when you give sadaqa, so you get rewarded for it - not only does He give you back what you gave away, but **He gives you much, much more.** The Prophet (saw) also said that giving in charity never makes the amount of money you have, less. **SO GIVING IN CHARITY, DOESN'T MAKE YOU POORER.**

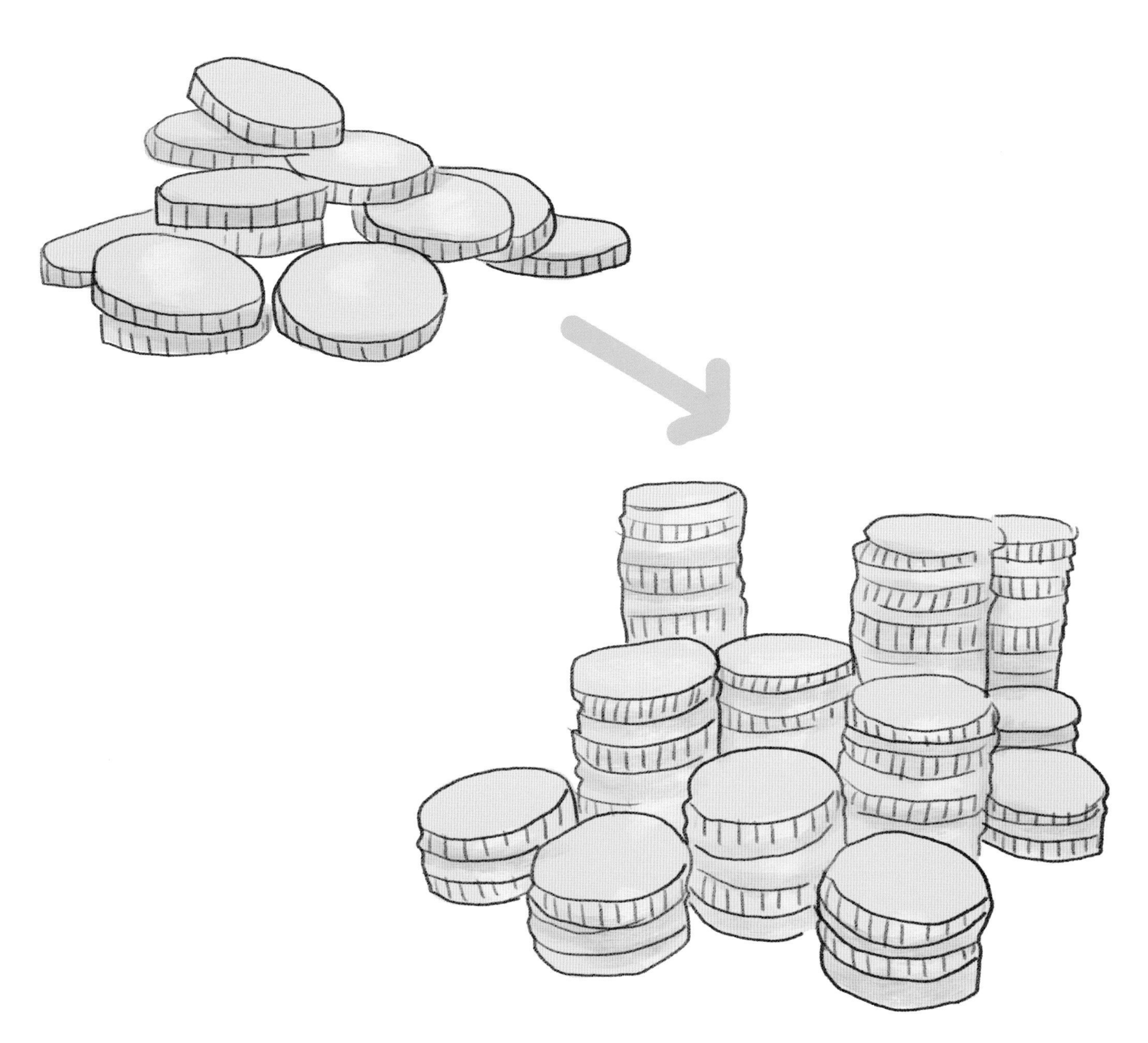

Saff

Saff is the Arabic word for row. We usually talk about saffs when we are praying together in jamaat, and we have to make the rows nice and straight. We stand shoulder to shoulder!

Sahaba

The sahaba were the friends and family of the Prophet (saw), or anyone who had met him, believed in his message, and died as a Muslim, too. The word sahaba is an Arabic word, and it means 'companions.'

We say a little tiny dua after we say the name of any companion of the Prophet (saw). We say radi-Allahu-anhu (may Allah be pleased with him) or anha (with her, if it's a lady or a girl). They all lived a long, long time ago, before there were cars, or planes or phones. People used to ride camels and horses.

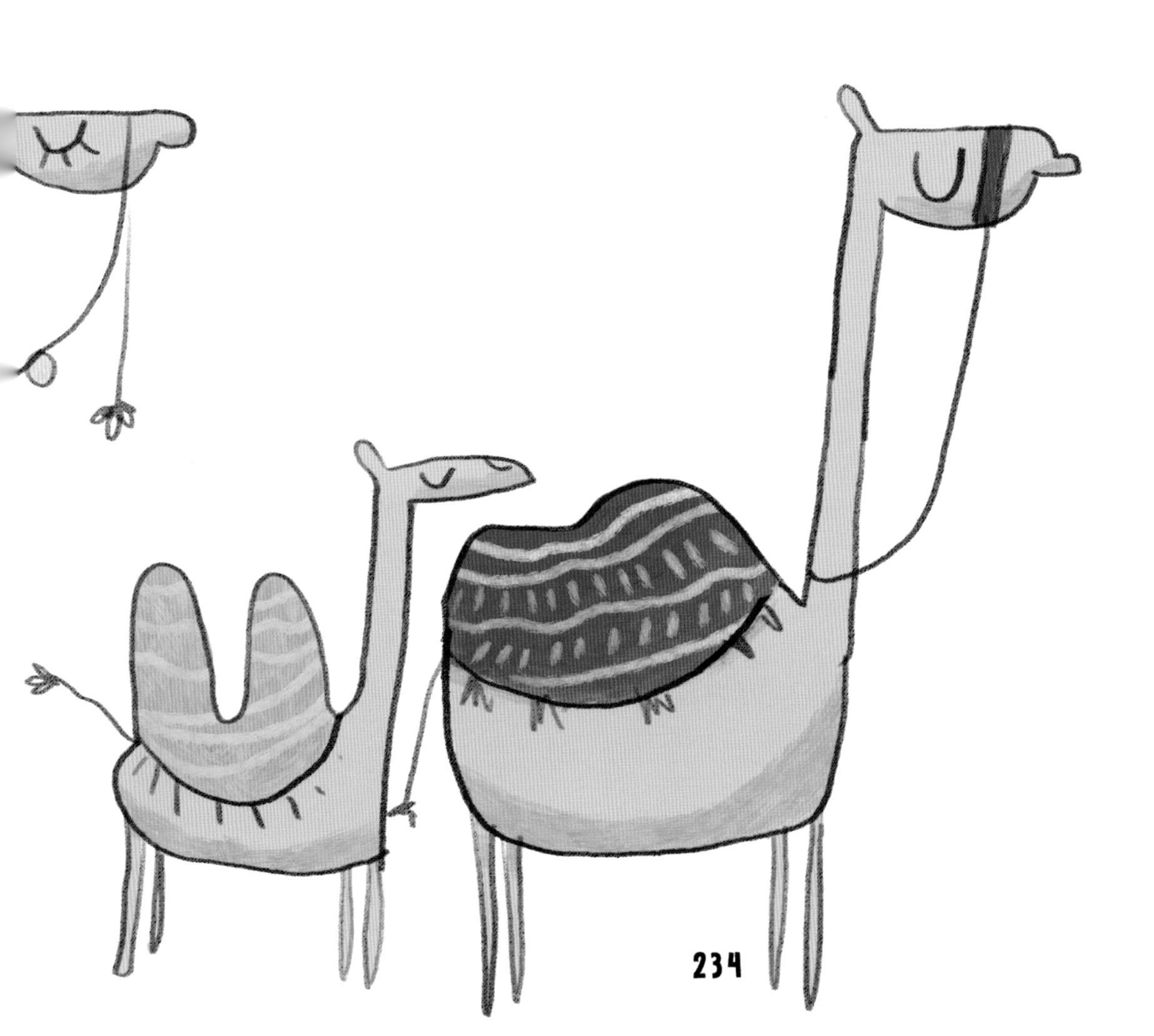

Some of the sahaba that were very close to the Prophet (saw) are; **Khadijah Bint Khawailid, Abu Bakr as-Siddiq, Ali Bin Abu Talib, Omar Bin Khattab, Aisha Bint Abu Bakr, Fatimah Bint Muhammad, Uthman Ibn Affan (ra).**

Ali: I know some of those names! Some of those names are the people who became the caliphs (rulers after the Prophet [saw]), Migo, and some of them are the wives of the Prophet (saw), and Fatimah (ra) is his daughter.

Migo: Yes, that's right my honey-covered cone! They were the closest people to the Prophet (saw) and people with the greatest imaan.

Salaam

Salaam means '**peace**'. When Muslims meet each other, we say salaam, which means we are wishing peace on each other. Giving salaam increases love between people. The **sahaba** used to say salaam to each other all the time, even if they just went into the other room and came back. Imagine it! You're telling someone that you wish, you *really, really* wish, that they have peace. Peace means that nothing is troubling or harming them and they are not worried about things.

Ali: Some people say a long salaam, Migo. What's the difference?

Migo: Well it's really about how generous you are being. When you meet someone, you could give them one sweet, or two sweets or three sweets. One sweet is very nice, two are nicer and three are the nicest!

Asalamualaikum means peace be upon you. ●

Asalamualaikum **warahmatullah** means peace and mercy of Allah be upon you. ● ●

Asalamualaikum **warahmatullah** wabarakatuhu means peace and mercy and blessings of Allah be upon you. ● ● ●

There is a hadith about spreading salaam, where the Prophet (saw) was asked what the best thing in Islam is. He said, 'Feeding others and giving the greeting of salaam to those whom you know and those whom you do not know.'

Salah

Salah is the prayer that Muslims pray five times a day. It is the second pillar of Islam.
Here are the names and times of the prayers:

- Salat al-fajr: dawn, before sunrise, when most people are sleeping and have to wake up to pray.
- Salat al-zuhr: midday.
- Salat al-'asr: the late part of the afternoon
- Salat al-maghrib: just after sunset
- Salat al-'isha: between sunset and midnight

As you can see, the times depend on where the sun is.

When the Prophet (saw) went on the Israa' journey, (see Israa' and mi'raj), he was given the gift of salah, by Allah.

Salah is prayed in units. Some of the units are fard (see Fard), which means that they are the ones we absolutely must pray, each day, when we reach the age. Some units are sunnah (see Sunnah), which means you can pray the salah without praying those units, but it is best to, and out of the sunnah units, some are more important to do - those are the ones in pink.

Prayer	Sunnah units before fard	Fard Units	Sunnah units after fard
Fajr	2	2	0
Dhuhr	4	4	2
Asr	4	4	0
Maghrib	0	3	2
Isha	4	4	2 plus 3 Witr

When we pray salah, we face the **Qibla,** which is the direction of the **Kaaba.** (see Qibla).

Ali: And we have to wear clean clothes, and pray on a clean mat!

Migo: Yes, we have to make sure our clothes, our body and the place where we are praying are clean. We don't have to use a mat, as long as we are sure that the area is clean.

Ali: What if I just dropped some purple grape juice on my top just before I go into the mosque, Migo?

Migo: Good question, Ali. And you do manage to do that more often than expected! Well, things like juice on your clothes make you look messy and dirty, but actually you can still pray in them. There are other really dirty things, which you have to be really careful about, because you absolutely can't pray with clothes that have that sort of dirt on.

Ali: Like what?

Migo: Like, blood, vomit, urine (pee) and faeces (poo).

Ali: Yuck! I never have those on my clothes anyway!

Migo: Good to know, my coconut cream cookie!

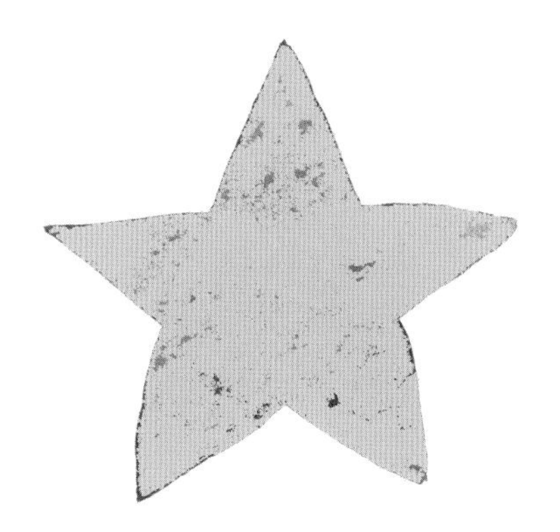

Shaytan

Shaytan is a very annoying creature, because he plays tricks on us all day long. He whispers to us to try to make us do bad things, or even to stop us doing good things, and he enjoys it!
He isn't scary, because only Allah has power and strength over all things, including us. The Shaytan is just very tricky and we need to know how to annoy him right back and scare him away in seconds!

Ali: How, Migo?
Migo: It's so easy. Just say,

A'udhoo-biLLah

MIN ASH SHAYTAN-IR RAJIM

Also:

When I am about to get angry, I say a'udhoo-billah.

When I stumble or fall, I say bismillah.

When I think of doing something bad, I do something good instead.

When I'm about to tell a lie, I tell the truth instead.

When I think I am better than someone else, I say astaghfirullah.

When I don't feel like giving money in charity, I give even more.

All those things make Shaytan miserable and weak.

ALi: So it's easy to beat the Shaytan if you know how, right?
Migo: Right, my smarty pants!

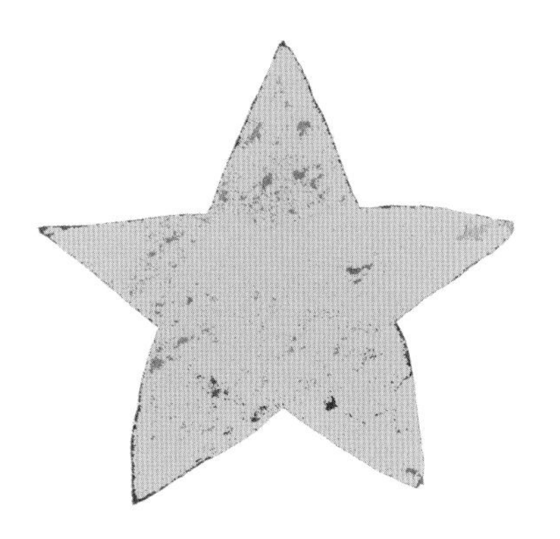

Subhan-Allah

We say Subhan-Allah when we see or hear something that makes us realise that **Allah is completely perfect and absolutely glorious.**
We say it when we look at the things He has created, like *beautiful* sceneries with oceans and mountains and trees.

We also say it when something happens that is really *amazing,* or *surprising,* for example, if
you hear about how fast an animal can run.

Ali: Can I say Subhan-Allah about how fast you can drive?
Migo: Hahaha, yes my quick-thinking cherry!

Sujood

Sujood is the Arabic word for prostration, which means kneeling down on your hands and knees and putting your face on the floor. You know it, because we do it in our salah. It's the part of the salah when we say,

'Subhaana Rabbi Al Alaa.'
'Glory be to my Lord, Most High.'

You put your face on the floor for Allah, because He is glorious and the *only one* who you would ever make sujood to. You feel humble in front of Him.

Sunnah

Sunnah is the word we use to speak about the way of the Prophet (saw). The way he did things and what he said we should do. We follow the sunnah, or the way the Prophet (saw) did things, because if he did them or asked us to do them, then they **absolutely must be the best way to do things.**
When you do something because it's a sunnah, you get **reward** from Allah, but it's not something you definitely have to do. Some sunnah actions are more important, because the Prophet (saw) did them all the time.

SUNNAH

Ali: In my salah, I do my sunnahs sometimes. Is that the same thing, Migo?

Migo: Yes, in salah, we pray some extra bits that are called sunnah, because the Prophet (saw) did them.

Ali: What else did he do that I do?

Migo: Some of the duas that you say, are duas that he used to say. Like the one for when you leave the house. Even smiling is a sunnah, because there was nobody who smiled more than the Prophet (saw). Also, leaving space in your belly when you eat, only eating and drinking when sitting down and only saying good things or keeping quiet, are all sunnah.

Ali: Wow, I'll never eat till I feel sick, again!

Migo: Haha, good idea!

Surah

A surah is a chapter from the Qur'an, for example, Surah Ikhlaas. They are different lengths. The longest is Surah Al-Baqara and the shortest is Al-Kauther. Surahs are numbered and sorted into 30 sections, or parts, of the Qur'an, called a juz.

You should try to learn as many surahs as you can and you can recite them wherever you are.

Ali: Sometimes we recite surahs in the car, don't we, Migo?
Migo: We sure do, my twinkly star.

Tahajjud

Tahajjud is a special, extra prayer that is prayed in the night, after getting some sleep. You pray it 2 units at a time. It's best to do it in the last part of the night, which is a very special time of the night.

There is a hadith which tells us that the Prophet (saw) said that the Lord (Allah) comes down every night, to the lowest heaven (skies above us), when one third of the night is left and He says, **"Who will call to Me so that I can answer them? Who will ask me for something so that I may give it to them? Who will ask me to forgive them so that I may forgive them?"**

Do you see how ***SPECIAL*** that is? Allah comes down in a way that fits Him (because He is not like us), ready, waiting for us to just ask Him for what we need! So if you ever have a problem, or need something, the best thing to do is to pray tahajjud and talk to Allah.

ALi: Wow, Migo, tahajjud is an amazing prayer and I want to do it!

Migo: Yes, my cherry nut button, the Prophet (saw) said that the tahajjud prayer is the best prayer after the five prayers of the day, that we must pray. It really is amazing.

ALi: Wake me up tonight, Migo. I'm going to do it.

Migo: OK, Ali, I will. Night, night.

Takbeer, Tahleel, Tahmeed, Tasbih

Takbeer is to say that Allah is great, by saying Allahu Akbar.

Tahleel is to say, with belief, that Allah is one - La ilaaha ill-Allah.

Tahmeed is to thank Allah and praise Him, by saying Alhamdulillah.

Tasbih is glorifying Allah, saying how perfect He is by saying Subhan Allah.

In the **first ten days of Dhul Hijjah**, we do a lot of Takbeer, Tahleel, Tahmeed and Tasbih. There is great **REWARD** from Allah and very many **BLESSINGS** for people who often say these words.

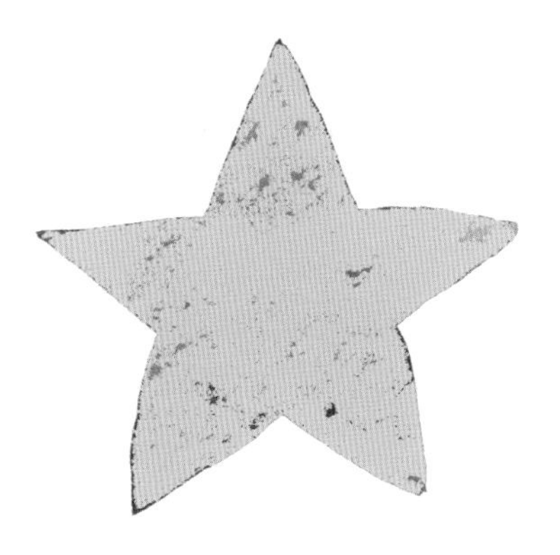

Taqwa

Having taqwa means being aware of Allah and so acting in a way that He wants us to. That means *knowing that Allah is near you and is watching you and listening to you at every moment of your day!* And because you know that, you behave in the best way.

Ali: Like when I behave extra good when Nani comes over, because I know she is watching me?

Migo: Haha, cheeky boots. Yes, just like that, except we do it for Allah. Even though we can't see Allah there, like we see Nani, we have to remember that He is seeing everything.

Tawakkul

If you **completely trust in Allah and His plan** for how things are going to happen, you have something very special, called tawakkul. You have tawakkul because you understand that *Allah knows* things that you don't know, so **He knows what is better for us and He will take care of us in the way that only He knows is best.**

Allah says in the Qur'an, that if someone relies on Him, He will be enough for him. That means that the person who knows that he/she *doesn't need anyone but Allah*, and that Allah is there for him/her to help and give, then **Allah will be all they ever need** because there is nothing that Allah won't do for someone like that.

Tawakkul

Tawheed

Tawheed means something really special but really simple. It means believing that Allah is **ONE**. That there is only **ONE** God, which is Allah, and that He doesn't need any one to help Him. It means to believe that there is **nothing like Allah.** He is completely different to everything and everyone.

Ali: I can't imagine what He looks like Migo, because everything I imagine is like something I've seen already.

Migo: You're right my snowflake, you can't imagine Him, but you will get to see Him one day, in-sha-Allah.

Ali: I can't wait, Migo!

Migo: Me too!

Umrah

Just like Hajj, Umrah is a journey we make to Makkah, for Allah. But it's different to Hajj, and can be done at any time of the year.

The actions that are done for Umrah are also done during Hajj. Umrah is not a pillar of Islam, like Hajj is, but it brings **so much reward, that we should do it as often as we can.**

The first step for doing Umrah is getting into ihram (see Hajj). You can do that at one of the Miqat, or before passing the Miqat. The Miqat are the places on the way to Makkah, where you get into ihram. For example, if you were leaving from the UK for Umrah, you could get into ihram from home in the UK, if you wanted to.

You have to recite the talbiya (see Hajj) when you get into ihram and carry on reciting it now and then, during your journey.

When you get to Makkah, you go towards the Kaaba to do something called tawaaf. This is walking around the Kaaba, anticlockwise, seven times. You start doing this at the *black stone* of the Kaaba. While you are doing the tawaaf, you should be **thinking about Allah** and making dhikr (see Dhikr).

After the tawaaf, the pilgrim (person doing Umrah or Hajj) does something called the sa'ay. For this part, you walk **SEVEN TIMES FROM MOUNT SAFA, TO MOUNT MARWA**.

ALi: Migo, oh Migo, wait! That's from the stories of the prophets! That's what Prophet Ibrahim's (as) wife, Hajar (as) did when she was looking for water for baby Ismail (as).

Migo: Perfect! Exactly right, my lychee juice in a cup! That's why we have to do that when we do Umrah, to remember the struggle that she went through.

ALi: Is Umrah good for us, Migo? Like apples are good for us?

Migo: Haha, yes but it's actually good for our imaan (see Imaan) rather than just our body. And the most special thing is that when we are doing Umrah or Hajj, we are Allah's guests. Imagine that!

ALi: Woah, Migo. Is that true?

Migo: Yes, Allah chooses people, from all over the world, to go to His house, the Kaaba; so when you are there, you are His guest. Also, Allah forgives people for the wrong things that they did, and gives them lots of reward when they do Umrah.

Wajib

For some people, wajib is another word that is used to describe something that is fard (see Fard). Others believe it is only a teeny tiny bit less important than fard. Either way, if something is wajib, it's so important to do that you should never miss it. An example is the witr units of prayer you pray with Isha Salah.

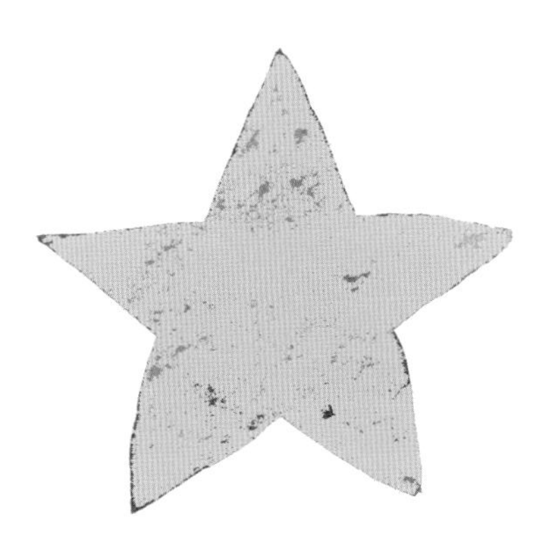

Wudu

Wudu is when you go in the bathroom and do lots of splashing around with water.

Ali: Hahaha, no it's not, Migo! It's when you make yourself all clean and ready to be able to pray. You have to wash your hands, mouth, face, arms, and wipe your head and feet!

Migo: Haha, well YOU do make a mess when you do all that, my little mess pot.

Wudu is very **special**, because if you do it properly, it washes away your sins (bad actions). The more times we have done wudu, the more our faces will shine bright when we meet Allah, and even the Prophet (saw) will be able to recognise that we are from his people.

Zakat

Zakat is giving money to the poor and needy, but unlike charity that we *choose* to do, this type of giving is a fantastic thing that every Muslim (who has the money) *must* do, because it is one of the Pillars of Islam.

Zakat is very special, because it helps us remember that everything we have, belongs to Allah. He's the one who gave it to us in the first place! That's why we should use the things we have, to help others, and we should be very thankful that Allah gave them to us.

Zakat

You might think that giving away some of your money would leave you with less, but it's not really like that. Gardeners trim away some parts of a plant, even the pretty flowers, so that the plant can grow even more. That's exactly what happens to our money when we give zakat.

ALi: So how much money do we have to give, Migo?

Migo: Good question my cinnamon bagel! Once you have a certain amount of money, you have to give 2.5% of that.

ALi: What's 2.5%? That sounds small.

Migo: It is. For example, if you had one hundred cupcakes, you would have to give away two and a half of them.

ALi: I wish I had one hundred cupcakes!

Migo: Haha, me too!

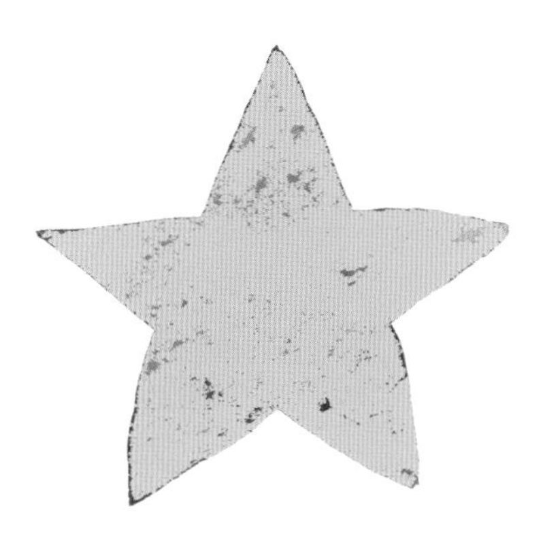

Zamzam

Zamzam is the name of the water from the Zamzam well in the holy mosque, in **Makkah**, where the **Kaaba** is.

When Prophet Ismail (as) was just a baby he was in a valley with his mother Hajar (as). There was no water, food, fruit or even trees. He was crying because he was very thirsty and his mother was running from mountain to mountain to look for water. **She knew everything would be just fine, because Allah would look after them, and she was right!** Angel Jibreel (as) came and hit the earth and a spring of water started flowing. It was Zamzam! Since then there has been plenty of Zamzam flowing, for millions of people to drink!

Zamzam water is not just normal water. It is special and there is no other water like it. Because it has special things in it, it is extremely refreshing and can **heal** people who are ill. It is a huge **BLESSING** to drink Zamzam.

ALi: Migo, some people bring Zamzam from Makkah for us!

Migo: That's right, my rainbow ray, they want to share the blessings with us and give us a chance to have it even if we can't go there.

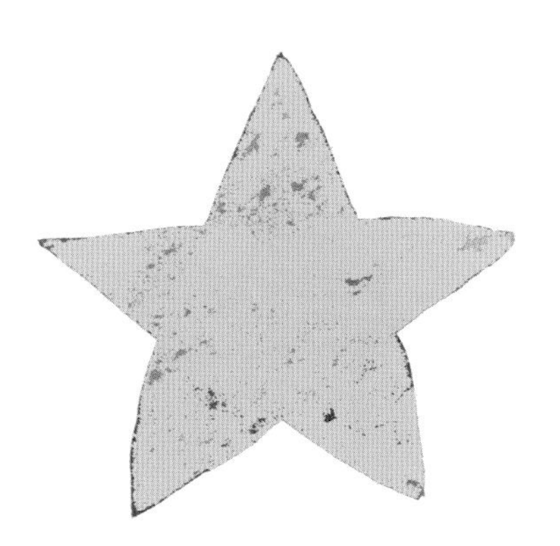

A small gem for you...

How to feel OK if you wanted something, but didn't get it...

Sometimes, when people want something, they can't stop thinking about it and carry the 'wanting' around with them like a huge, heavy weight. Even though they can't do anything about it. And if they don't get it, the 'wanting' gets even bigger, and heavier, and then they carry that around too.

But, you don't have to carry your 'wanting'. You can just pass it to Allah T'aala to carry for you. Because He's the only one that can give you that thing, anyway. That way, you can try for the thing you want, without the worrying.

And not worry about the thing, if you didn't get it.

It's pointless wanting something Allah thought best not to give you, anyway.

Taken from 'The Young Muslim's Mindful Book of Wellbeing', by Zanib Mian

Other fantastic titles by Zanib Mian

Visit muslimchildrensbooks.co.uk

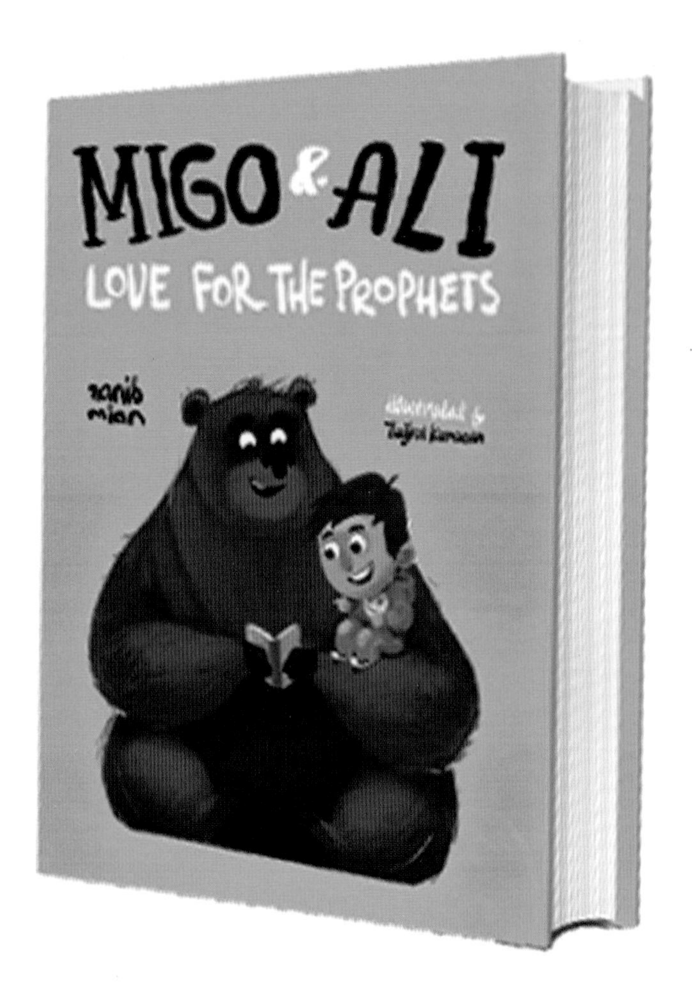

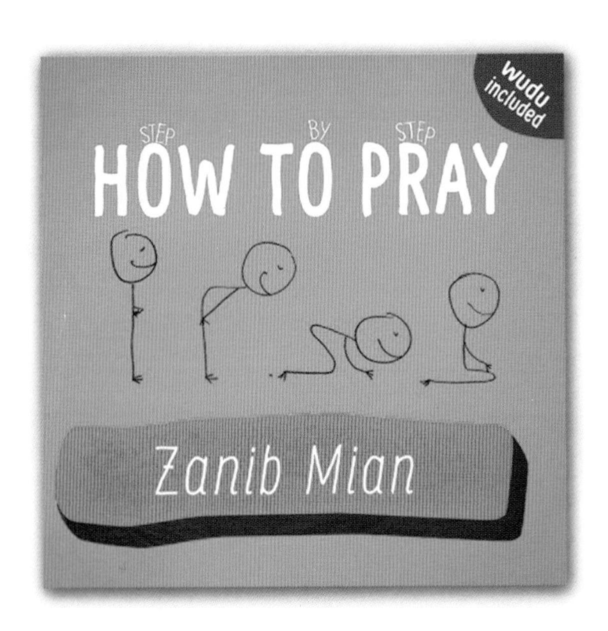
wudu included
STEP BY STEP
HOW TO PRAY
Zanib Mian

The Young Muslim's Mindful Book of Wellbeing
Zanib Mian

It MUST have been you!
Zanib MIAN

My Dad's Beard
Zanib Mian
Laura Ewing

Musa & Friends Say Bismillah
Zanib Mian
Illustrated by Daniel Hills

Musa & Friends Say Alhamdulilah
Zanib Mian
Illustrated by Daniel Hills

Musa & Friends Go to the Masjid
Zanib Mian
Illustrated by Daniel Hills

Musa & Friends Do Ramadan
Zanib Mian
Illustrated by Daniel Hills

MIGO
ALI
Migo
ALI
HI